Off Duty Holsters:

Concealed Weapons
Carry For Cops

A book by

Michael W. Weissberg

WHITE MOUNTAIN PUBLISHING CO.

MIAMI, FLORIDA

WHITE MOUNTAIN PUBLISHING CO.

MIAMI, FLORIDA

First edition
Library of Congress Cataloging-in-Publication Data
Weissberg, Michael.

Off Duty Holsters: Concealed Carry For Cops by Michael Weissberg – 1st ed.

Library of Congress Control Number:
PCN 2011923625
ISBN-10 098348662X
ISBN-13 9780983486626

10 9 8 7 6 5 4 3 2 1

Book design by Michael Weissberg

Cover Photo by Michael Weissberg

Printed in the United States of America

Acknowledgements

Sam Andrews, a man truly born in the wrong century. Sam, you are an artisan, a gentleman, and a genius.

Grandmaster Bram Frank, a truly world-class martial artist, and possibly the best tactical knife teacher in the world today. Thank you for being my friend.

Ed Gottlieb, you are an inspired teacher.

Lastly, to my wife, Erika B. Weissberg: thanks for being my wife, and being the mother to our son, Dean Bennett Bacon Weissberg.

Dedication

During his 22 years of dedicated service to the Miami Police Department, Sgt. Angel Calzadilla performed honorably as hostage negotiator, department spokesman, and executive assistant to the police chief.

Sgt. Calzadilla once pulled a suicidal woman hanging from a ledge on the 52nd-floor of a downtown hotel high-rise to safety after talking her into letting him get close.

During the Elian Gonzalez international custody dispute, Calzadilla stressed the need for keeping civil order, but spoke passionately about the conflict many Cuban American officers felt. Angel was my cousin (by marriage).

Sergeant Angel Calzadilla succumbed to Cystic Fibrosis and drifted into an eternal sleep. He was 48 years of age.

In memory of
Sgt. Angel Calzadilla
City of Miami Police Department
22 Year Police Veteran

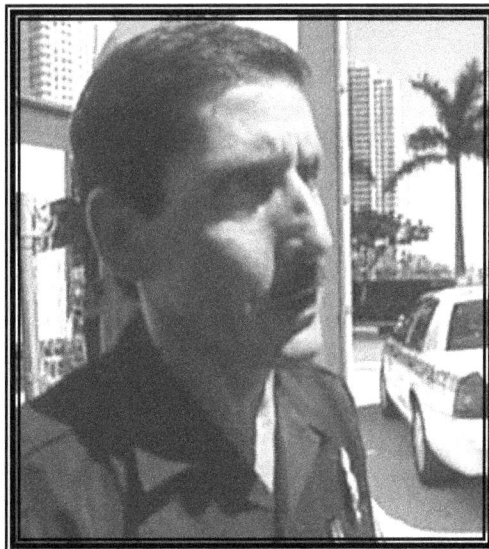

Also by
Michael W. Weissberg:

Honor, Glory, Respect:
Conducting Police Funerals

Processing Environmental Crime Scenes

The Firearm as a Martial Arts Weapon

What Every Cop Must Know:
Tactical Preparation for the Worst Day of Your Life

About the Author
Michael W. Weissberg

Michael Weissberg began his career as an educator in 1988. A graduate of the University of Miami, Weissberg holds Master's degrees in Education, Criminal Justice and Psychology.

Professor Weissberg has taught on the undergraduate level at Miami Dade College, St. Thomas University, and Florida International University, and graduate school at Nova Southeastern University.

Weissberg has served as a Police Officer, Administrative Officer, Crime Scene Investigator, Police Detective, and a Police Sergeant, and Acting Lieutenant. In the Private Investigations and Security Industry he has served as Assistant Chief and Director.

Michael Weissberg was awarded an instructor's certificate, school license, and black belt in Filipino Arnis and the title of Guro by Grandmaster Bram Frank, and affirmed by Professor Remy A. Presas, and subsequently promoted and named personal student of Grandmaster Bram Frank.

To Honor Fallen
Police Officers:

The National Law Enforcement Officers Memorial is the nation's monument to law enforcement officers who have died in the line of duty. Please donate.

If you would like to contribute by phone,
please call 202-737-3400.

If you would like to contribute
by Mail, please write:

NLEOMF
901 E Street NW, Suite 100
Washington, DC 20004-2025
info@nleomf.org

The Police Officer's Assistance Trust was founded in 1989 as a nonprofit support organization for the law enforcement community of Miami-Dade County, Florida. To make a donation in honor of

Sgt. Angel Calzadilla
City of Miami Police Department

Contact:
Police Officer's Assistance Trust
1030 NW 111 Avenue,
Miami, Florida 33172
305.594.6662
Email: poatoffice@msn.com

A PORTION OF THE SALE OF THIS BOOK WILL BE DONATED TO POAT FOR THE FAMILIES OF OFFICRS KILLED IN LINE OF DUTY IN MIAMI-DADE COUNTY, FLORIDA.

Introduction

You will read things here that may be unpopular, may make you angry, and may save your life. This book is for you; not because I know so much, because I don't. It's because we know so little, are our own worst enemies, and because we forget so much.

This book isn't designed to be a "how-to" book on tactics or shooting, but one would be remiss not to mention the difference between cover and concealment. Concealment simply makes it harder for an assailant to see you. Bushes are concealment; bullets go through bushes and make you dead. Cover makes it harder for an assailant to shoot you. A blue freestanding USPS mailbox or a car is cover.

Taking a good position behind an engine block is preferable to hiding. Having good equipment which is well maintained is essential. Practicing with your equipment is important. Training can save your life.

As I said in my last book: The best we can do, is the least we can do.

Non soleus, (Never alone)
The Author

Guns and Shooting

Shooting is a skill that degrades over time. Officers should shoot their guns every month, and practice drawing from the holster weekly. This is not something that is debated.

Most officers shoot only once a year and never practice drawing. This is due to laziness. A civilian would think that an officer would want to practice with the arm that might save his life, but most cops simply don't practice.

There is a story that is very common in the police world. Ron (name changed) was a thirty-four year veteran. Ron probably should have retired years ago, but after the death of his wife, Ron simply had nothing else to do.

Ron never had any kids, due to an accident that happened when he was a kid. The sixty-three year old entered the police department after serving in the Marine Corps. Ron wasn't a drinker, but poured a bit of Irish whiskey into his glass every now and then. Ron didn't bowl, and had few hobbies.

Ron figured a retirement would be boring. Most of Ron's friends had retired and died soon after. Ron figured he wasn't ready to sit around the house in his robe and do nothing just yet.

Ron was found shot to death in a dark warehouse. Ron's police issued .38 special Smith and Wesson 4-inch barreled, model 66 revolver was in his right hand. The old police revolver probably should have been traded in for a semiautomatic pistol a decade earlier. Ron simply liked the old "wheelgun" and wanted to keep using it

The crime scene investigator noted that the gun was frozen and the action could not be functioned. The CSI had to take the gun to a departmental armorer to take the gun apart. The rounds in the gun were a semi-jacketed hollow point of a brand the department had gone away from over six years prior. The rounds had green verdigris on them.

It was determined that Gene (name changed), a thirty-two year veteran, and the Chief Range Officer at the departmental shooting range, had simply signed off on Ron for years. Ron probably had not fired that gun for over a decade. Gene admitted that he and Ron would sit and drink coffee and swap stories when Ron came to the range every six months to qualify.

Ron's funeral was attended by thousands. Shopkeepers, housewives, politicians, firemen, police officers, students, and teachers, lined up to file past the kindly old veteran's casket. Ron was a big man. At over six feet and nearly 275 pounds, Ron was a big muscular guy who had gone a little soft.

The department's brass spent hours eulogizing the old veteran, who was the last of his breed. They said he died valiantly with his gun in his hand. They never told the mourners that Ron's gun was as useless as a paperweight.

The day of the funeral, an appropriately cold and rainy January 29th, Gene quietly retired and did his final paperwork at the nearly deserted city hall, while his old friend was buried. Every year on January 29th, Gene visits the grave and pours a bit of Irish whiskey on the mound to salute the old war-horse.

Gene had a few good years left in him, drinking coffee and teaching "slick- sleeved rookies" how to shoot, but he "pulled the pin" early and retired. Gene sits in front of the television, in his old robe, watching cop shows and reading gun magazines. Gene hasn't shot a gun since Ron's death. Ron had a few good years left in him too. Ron's death was needless, pointless, and a damn shame.

Ron wouldn't train, even for free. Many new cops will spend hundreds of dollars on firearms, but refuse to spend their own money on training. Ammunition, range fees, and training tuition are cheap compared to the cost of hospitals, funerals, and lost wages.

There are several good civilian firearms instructors out there, including Ken Hackathorn, Ed Gottlieb, James Bigwood, and Andy Stanford; there are big fancy outfits like *Thunder Ranch* and *Gunsite*. Some instructors will run a three gun course, where officers can transition from an AR15 to a handgun or from a handgun to a shotgun. You can attend famous programs such as the *Lethal Force Institute*.

Most cops wouldn't give their hard-earned dollars to these civilian instructors, because they are not cops. When they have the opportunity to train with police instructors, they either complain about it, or just don't listen. Cops are among the hardest people to teach. Most cops get to train for free, but never put in for training.

Schools on tactics, weapons choice, and marksmanship are available to civilians and officers alike. The National Rifle Association can refer interested persons to police, security, and civilian courses all designed to hone skills.

Firearms
Glossary of Gun Terms

Although a glossary often comes at the end of a book, I have included the glossary of gun terms here so that the reader will understand all terminology that is used in the section.

Action: A group of moving parts used to load, fire, and unload the firearm.

Barrel: The tube down which the projectile(s) travel.

Caliber: The measure of the internal bore diameter of a gun's barrel from land to land, which is expressed in hundredths of an inch, thousandths of an inch, or in millimeters.

Cartridge: The primer, powder, case and projectile that are used in modern firearms.

Clip: A metal strip that holds rounds together. Not a magazine.

Double Action: In addition to releasing the hammer or striker, DA triggers cock the hammer or striker.

Gauge: The measure of the internal diameter of a shotgun's bore; the number of balls of lead the diameter of the bore equal to one pound. If it takes 12 balls of lead the diameter of the bore to make a pound of lead, then the gun is a 12 Ga.

Grips: The part of the handgun the shooter's hand wraps

around.

Hollow Point: The solitary metal projectile which is sent down-range, which has a hollow cavity for greater expansion.

Lands: The original part of the bore where no rifling exists.

Less lethal: Ammunition or devices designed to subdue rather than kill, such as rubber bullets, beanbag loads, TASERs, and pepper spray.

Magazine: An ammunition feeding device. Not to be confused with a Clip. Most guns have a magazine rather than a clip.

Muzzle: The end of a gun's barrel from which the projectile emerges.

Night Sights: The mechanical sighting system which uses glass tubes full of tritium (heavy-heavy hydrogen, or T3), coated on the inside with phosphorus, and encased in aluminum and rubber. The decay of the tritium puts off photons of light.

Non-Shooting Hand: the weak hand or non-dominant hand that the shooter naturally does not prefer to shoot with.

Pistol: A semiautomatic hand gun which stores ammunition in a magazine. Not to be confused with a revolver.

Revolver: A handgun with a revolving cylinder, which holds the cartridges. Each time the trigger is pulled, the cylinder rotates and allows a fresh cartridge to be fired.

Rifling: The cutting or broaching of spiral grooves into the interior surface of a gun in order to cause the bullet to spin.

Safety: A mechanical device which can and will fail, which is used to supplement your own safe gun handling; designed to prevent the gun from firing unintentionally.

Semi-automatic: A gun which, when the trigger is pulled and the chamber is loaded, will fire one round, eject the spent casing, and chamber a new round.

Shooting Hand: the strong hand or dominant hand that the shooter naturally prefers to shoot with.

Sights: The mechanical sighting system which usually comes with the firearm. It is so called to distinguish it from laser sights, red dot sights, and scoped sights.

Single Action: A single-action firearm has a hammer that is not actuated by the trigger. The hammer may be cocked by hand, or in a pistol, by racking the slide, or by the rearward movement of the slide after each shot is fired.

Strong Hand: the shooting hand or dominant hand that the shooter naturally prefers to shoot with.

Strong Side: A term used to describe the shooting hand side of the body; the side corresponding to the dominant hand.

TASER: An electroshock device that uses electrical current to disrupt voluntary control of muscles. TASER is an acronym for a fictional weapon: Thomas A. Swift's Electric Rifle.

Trigger: Pulling the trigger releases the striker or allows the hammer to fall, causing the firing pin to strike the primer.

Trigger Guard: The hoop encircling the area around the trigger.

Weak Hand: The non-shooting hand or non-dominant hand that the shooter naturally does not prefer to shoot with.

Weak Side: A term used to describe the non-shooting hand side of the body; the side corresponding to the non-dominant hand.

Off Duty Carry &
Gun Choice

This may be controversial, but I would *never* recommend a single action "cocked and locked" gun for anyone, law enforcement or otherwise, in this day and age. This is neither "the military" nor the "OK corral". I should mention that "the military" did away with the 1911 Government model.

Many good manufacturers are making and selling Cold Government clones: Strayer-Tripp, Les Baer, Remington, Springfield Armory, Smith and Wesson, Sig Sauer, and Norinco, just to name some. They make great range guns, they are fun to shoot, and they are great sellers. They are accurate and dependable. They are also outdated, outmoded, and obsolete.

The Glock Model 17 was introduced in 1983 by Gaston Glock, an inventor and founder of Glock GmbH, in Deutsch-Wagram, Austria. Glock, like many other major gun manufacturers, wanted to bid on the contract to provide 25,000 9mm semi-automatic combat handguns to the Austrian Army.

The other manufacturers centered their designs on earlier Browning designs and brought the same old hat to the ring.

Glock, who had never designed a gun before, invented a new safe-action system with soft recoil, and low weight through the use of space-age polymers that are stronger than steel at only 14% of the weight. The gun also would not freeze to your hand. Urban legend has it that Glock got the idea from a doorknob he designed when his hand froze to a doorknob and he had to pee on it to escape!

The Glock Model 17 was the 17th patent that Gaston Glock owned, and so the numeration of the models began with 17, 18, 19, and so on.

Since their introduction in the United States in 1986 with the City of Miami Police Department, Glock pistols have been adopted as issue weapons for more than an estimated 60% of the law enforcement agencies in America, and are in use world-wide by law enforcement and military units. The other major contenders are the Beretta 92 and the Sig Sauer P220, P226, and P229.

Glocks were called "Plastic Guns", and "Combat Tupperware". Urban legend had it that a Miami Cop left his gun on the car's dashboard and when he came back, the gun had melted! This is obviously a foolish, ridiculous story; where would this officer have gone off to without his gun, and why put it on the dashboard in the first place? With a thermal breakaway of over 1400°, the officer's patrol car would have had to have been on fire for this to be true.

Another legend had it that the Glock could go through metal detectors and X-ray machines. At 83% steel, the gun is easily detected, and is not a "terrorist weapon", or a "ceramic gun", despite Bruce Willis's character in the movie "Die Hard", and his fictional "Glock 7", which never existed. Even the US Congress got into the fray, and tried to ban importation of the Glock. Congress very nearly outlawed the importation of the "ceramic Glock 7" which was never invented!

I was one of the first writers to X-ray a Glock 17, and I published an article for Glock USA with the X-ray photo. See Weissberg, M. (1995): "Myths About The Glock." *The Glock Report.* Spring. Pg. 3. For more on this article.

The next set of urban myths to come out, were that the gun had "no safety", or that the safety was "on the trigger". All guns made in the USA or imported into the USA since 1968 have a safety. Glock employs three internal safety mechanisms, all activated via the trigger mechanism, that prevent the gun from firing if the gun is dropped on the muzzle or the butt, or if an ear of the leather holster gets into the trigger guard during re -holstering. The Glock does not have a user-manipulated button or lever, such as the Browning or Colt.

Those things the media and the Colt groupies considered to be design flaws in Glock pistols are now considered to be selling points. Individual Glocks have fired over one million rounds, fired when under water, crusted with mud, and after having been buried in desert sand.

Glocks have been frozen in ice, then and fired. Glocks have been run over (with a primed case chambered) by trucks, dropped from several stories with a chambered round with no ill effects.

Glocks are among the toughest, most accurate handguns available, and will digest any ammunition without a "ramp and throat job".

Heckler & Koch, Colt, Ruger, Springfield Armory, Beretta, and Smith & Wesson have all produced polymer framed guns since those heady days in 1986, when these companies made fun of "plastic guns".

Compared to the 1911, there is no competition. The Glock is a more modern winner; it took 75 years to beat the venerable warhorse, but with my sincere apologies to Massad Ayoob, Clint Smith, Jeff Cooper, Dave Arnold, and the other gunwriting legends, you lose. The Glock wins.

I offer this question: Tomorrow at 5:00 PM, you will get

into a gunfight. You may bring anything you own. What will you bring? Some may answer that they would bring a Sig Sauer P226 in 9mm NATO with two spare magazines; some may answer that they would bring a Glock 21 in .45 ACP with a flashlight and a spare magazine; some may answer that they would bring a Glock 35 in .40 S/W caliber and a pair of hand-cuffs; some may answer that they would bring a Colt 1911 .45 tricked out by John Nowlin, 4 magazines, a Smith and Wesson M 640 Centennial .38 Special as a backup, and pack it all in a Sam Andrews Urban Safari rig.

My response to these choices is this: then do it! Why are you packing a Beretta .32 in a pocket holster or a Smith and Wesson M66 in an ankle holster, if this is not your first choice? You already know what you would carry if you were all ready to go serve a warrant, so why not carry that gun off duty?

Is it really easier to conceal a Glock 27 than it is to conceal a Glock 35? If you are carrying in a hip holster, they really aren't much different (see the photos later on in this book for comparison). Obviously, if you are carrying your Glock 27 in an ankle holster, there is a difference. In a shoulder holster, there really isn't.

Choice of Gun
and Caliber

This is the most hotly debated topic in the gun world. The Definitive Study by Evan P. Marshall & Edwin J. Sanow explores this topic very well, and gives the reader several options. The .45 ACP 1911 crowd would have you believe that a "cocked and locked" Government or Commander model is the only thing worth carrying.

The champions of this crowd are Clint Smith, Jeff Cooper, Louis Awerbuck, Massad Ayoob, and others who are fans of this gun. Now this is not to suggest that they don't like other guns and don't recommend other guns.

Sometimes "gun writers" (whose opinion is no better or worse than yours) give endorsement of guns that just happen to be advertised heavily in that very issue of the magazine. Just because someone is a writer, does not make them a messiah or prophet. The endorsement is lukewarm at best.

Gun writers write reviews and say "the XP4000 *should* be a good gun for defense" (the italics are mine for emphasis). This is called "damning with faint praise". The hypothetical writer has gone on record a hundred times stating he carries a Colt Government or Colt Commander, but then must endorse a gun he would never carry, since that gunmaker bought thousands of dollars of ad space in that very issue of that very magazine.

Allow me to mention that I was a "gun writer". I was a Senior Editor. I was an Editor-in-Chief. We did interesting things like wrote articles with our names on them, articles without our names on them, articles with "staff-written" on them, articles with several names on them, and articles with our *nom de plumes* on them. Major Nigel Kilpling, RASC (ret.), and Sergeant Michael W. Weissberg, (ret.) are one and the same. This is the first time this has been acknowledged publicly. Sorry, Nigel.

Nigel got fan mail, ran contests, and had a secretary. Nigel was also an invention of my diabolical mind, a combination of Majordomo Jonathan Quail Higgins III, Sergeant Major, RASC (ret.), holder of the Victoria Cross, a character from the TV show *Magnum PI*, and Major Ronald Shelley, of the 42nd Regiment of Foote (Royal Americans), and distinguished resident of South Miami.

Did I mention that many glossy gun magazines were seeded with soft-core porn money or skin mag money way back when? They just traded boobs for guns when they made some dough. Now people respect them. Beware of taking an individual "gun writer's" advice as gospel; it is nothing more than one man's opinion.

This may be controversial, and you may not like it, but I would never recommend a single action "cocked and locked" gun for anyone, law enforcement or otherwise, this day and age. This is neither the military, nor the "OK corral". I should mention that the military did away with the 1911 Government model.

Many good manufacturers are making and selling Colt Government clones: Strayer-Tripp, Les Baer, Remington, Springfield Armory, Smith and Wesson, Sig Sauer, and Norinco, just to name a few. Colt clones make great range guns, they are fun to shoot, and they are great sellers; one of my personal favorites was made by Safari Arms.

The Colt clones are accurate and dependable. They are range guns. Single-action guns are not for carry anymore. You will be sued and called names. They will say you were "looking to murder someone". No one will care that you were being carjacked. No one will care that you were being attacked. No one will care that you were being stabbed. You will pull defeat from the jaws of victory. You will turn a "good shoot" into a legal nightmare.

The only thing the jury will hear is that you were issued a perfectly fine modern gun by the police department and you *chose* not to carry it; they will only hear that you were "cocked and locked and ready to kill". And you will lose. And you will pay dearly. And you will suffer greatly.

Now many will call me an idiot, and disregard this opinion, but I carry a Glock 35 both on and off-duty. The G35 is a big gun, with a big sight radius; it holds a lot of rounds. The gun is accurate, and shoots a powerful round. That is what I want if I am going to be in a gunfight.

I won't get to choose the time and date. The only thing in my power is to make use of cover and concealment, try to have the element of surprise, place my shots well, rely on my training and equipment, and hope for the best.

When people complain and mention they can't wear a favorite jacket or shorts while concealing a big pistol, I offer this maxim:

"Don't change your gun; change your clothes."

Taking Action While
Off-Duty

Here is another section you may not like. A great number of police officers are shot by other police officers while taking action off-duty.

Orlando, FL, 2005: A University of Central Florida Police Officer and USMC veteran was fatally shot by an Orlando PD officer outside the Citrus Bowl.

A third person, not identified by authorities, remained hospitalized Sunday with a gunshot wound, officials said. Mario Jenkins, who had been working with State Division of Alcoholic Beverages and Tobacco (ABT) agents, died after being shot Saturday by an Orlando Reserve Police Officer.

Witnesses said the undercover officer broke up a gathering of students, who resisted his efforts. The agent then discharged a shot into the air. The OPD officer saw the undercover officer who was dressed in street clothes, and shot him several times. Photos captured officer Mario Jenkins with his gun drawn and an apparent police badge hanging around his neck moments before he was shot and killed.

The Florida Department of Law Enforcement report shows that Maj. Randy Mingo, Jenkins' supervisor, told FDLE investigators he asked Jenkins to wait for another officer before heading into a crowd of fans, but Jenkins said he was OK. There were no backup officers to watch Jenkins, no radios to call for help, no pepper spray, TASERS or batons to use instead of guns, on rowdy tailgaters suspected of underage drinking. "Hey, I don't have a radio, so if you hear me screaming . . . come and find me," Jenkins, joked to a colleague 15 minutes before he died.

New York, NY 2006: In a case of mistaken identity, police shot and critically wounded an off-duty officer as he pointed a gun at a suspect outside a restaurant. Eric Hernandez, 24, was hit three times and was hospitalized in extremely critical condition. The officer who pulled the trigger, a 20-year veteran of the force, was treated for trauma at another hospital.

Hernandez had been in line at a restaurant when he was assaulted by a half-dozen men. The fight was captured on a security camera. An employee called 911, and Hernandez, with his gun drawn, ran into the parking lot; he subdued one of the suspects, and when a patrol car arrived, was pointing his gun at a man on the ground.

Baltimore, MD, 2008: A veteran Baltimore City police officer was shot and killed by another officer Thursday morning after he walked out of a bar with brass knuckles to join a fight and later drew a handgun, police said.

Los Angeles, CA 2008: A Long Beach police officer on Wednesday shot and wounded an off-duty Los Angeles police officer who allegedly brandished a shotgun and ignored officers' orders to drop the weapon.

Harlem NY, 2009: A New York City police officer who had just gotten off duty was fatally shot late Thursday in East Harlem by a fellow officer who mistook him for an armed criminal.

St. Louis, MO, 2011: An off-duty sheriff's deputy was drunk when he was shot to death by St. Louis police on a city street in

February, according to toxicology tests.

What do these cases have to teach us? Remember, you don't have your equipment or uniform with you. I think you should let the on-duty guys handle most situations. Call it in, and let them take care of business. In each of these cases, an off-duty officer was shot due to misidentification (the first case was an on-duty plainclothes officer).

Some of the police officers died. In one case, a badge on a chain was not adequate. Like most, *I don't like to criticize dead cops.* Take the case of the 1986 FBI shootout in Sunniland, what is now Pinecrest, Florida, in Miami-Dade County.

On April 11, 1986 FBI Agents and two bank robbers exchanged gunfire in the most famous shootout in FBI history. Special Agents Jerry L. Dove and Benjamin P. Grogan were killed. The two murder suspects, William Russell Matix and Michael Lee Platt, were also killed. In addition, five FBI agents were wounded in the incident.

The robbers had a .223 caliber Ruger Mini 14 rifle, and a S&W M3000 12-gauge shotgun, a S&W M586 .357 Magnum revolver, and a Dan Wesson .357 Magnum revolver.

The FBI had five .38 caliber revolvers, three S&W M459 9mm pistols, and two Remington M870 12-gauge shotguns. Supervisory Special Agent Gordon McNeill, Special Agent Richard Manauzzi, Special Agent Benjamin Grogan, Special Agent Jerry Dove, Special Agent Edmundo Mireles, Jr., Special Agent John Hanlon, Special Agent Gilbert Orrantia, and Special Agent Ronald Risner, attempted to arrest the robbers. There were plenty of agents, and plenty of guns; the tactics were the issue.

Just prior to ramming the subjects' car, Manauzzi had

pulled out his service revolver and placed it on the seat; the impact opened his door and he lost his weapon. Hanlon also lost his .357 Magnum service revolver during the initial collision, though he was still able to fight with his Smith & Wesson Model 36 backup gun. The collision also knocked off Grogan's eye glasses, making it almost impossible for him to see.

In 2001, the Village of Pinecrest, Florida, which incorporated in 1996, honored the two agents by co-designating a portion of Southwest 82nd Avenue as Agent Benjamin Grogan Avenue and Agent Jerry Dove Avenue. Street signs and a historical marker commemorate the naming of the roadway in honor of the two agents.

After the shooting the families of Jerry Dove and Benjamin Grogan sued the estates of Platt and Matix for damages. The lawsuit was dismissed.

What was accomplished? The FBI went to Smith and Wesson 10mm pistols which were so universally hated, that they then went to the 10mm short, which they then renamed the .40 S/W which is the mathematical conversion from millimeters to hundredths of an inch.

I had the distinct honor of meeting and talking with Agent Hanlon at the 2001 street dedication. I am in no way faulting these brave men, but I must say these tactics were not the best. Changing tactics would have been better than replacing all of the arms with the 10 millimeter. Ultimately, we got the .40 S/W out of it, which replaces the universally loved 9mm NATO.

Still, *we don't like to criticize dead cops.*

NOTE: This material was supplemented from: Anderson, W. (1996): *Forensic Analysis of the April 11, 1986, FBI Firefight.* Boulder, CO: Pladin Press.

Off-Duty
Career Difficulties

These cases illustrate what happens to officers who had difficulties off-duty. I teach that you have to come out of the action with several things intact, *or you lose:*

- Mentally unharmed
- Physically unharmed
- Emotionally unharmed
- Financially unharmed
- Reputation unharmed
- Legally unharmed
- Family unharmed
- Department unharmed

Some examples from the news, of officers who did not come out of the action unharmed:

New York, NY, 2008: An off-duty police officer, apparently visiting relatives on Staten Island, was shot in the leg. Police believe it was during a robbery attempt in the Port Richmond section.

Las Vegas, NV, 2009: An off-duty Las Vegas Metro police officer was shot to death in an attempted robbery. North Las Vegas Police say Nettleton was attacked inside his garage by multiple suspects. A neighbor called police to report hearing several gunshots coming from the home. There was an exchange of gunfire between the suspects and Nettleton before the victim was shot. He was pronounced dead at the scene.

Chicago, IL, 2010: A veteran officer was found dead in his personal sport-utility vehicle. The officer was a 15-year veteran of the force, and was assigned to the SWAT team.

Chicago, IL, 2010: A 62-year-old Chicago police officer less than a month from retiring was killed early Sunday as he returned home from an overnight shift. Officer Michael Bailey was shot at outside his home; he was taken to the Hospital and pronounced dead there. Chicago officials say Bailey was cleaning his car when several people approached him and may have tried to steal the vehicle. No arrests have been made.

Philadelphia, PA, 2010: An off-duty Philadelphia police officer was in stable condition after being shot in the leg. According to police, the officer was shot in the thigh during an argument.

Washington DC, 2010: An off-duty U.S. Capitol Police officer was involved in a shooting in Prince Georges County, Maryland. The U.S. Capitol Police officer and a suspect exchanged gunfire. The officer was shot and transported to a hospital with non-life threatening injuries. The suspect was shot multiple times and transported to a hospital. A bystander was also treated for a graze wound and transported to a hospital.

Chicago, IL, 2010: Chicago off-duty Officer Thomas Wortham IV was gunned down at as he was leaving his parents' home. According to the Chicago Sun Times, he was approached by several men who tried to steal his motorcycle. His father, who is a retired Chicago police officer, shot two of the suspects, killing one and wounding the other, police said. Officer Wortham was shot in the head in the ensuing gunfire. He died shortly after midnight. It is woth mentioning that this man survived two tours of duty in Iraq, only to die in his own city.

Cincinnati, OH, 2010: An off-duty police officer was shot in the abdomen at a restaurant. Officer Thomas Owens was in the drive thru when some men started getting rowdy and Owens told them to settle down. When Owens left, one of the men shot him.

Miami-Dade, FL 2010: An off-duty police officer shot two men after a fight at a cash machine in Hialeah Gardens, police said. The Miami-Dade officer was withdrawing money from the ATM when he said three men pulled up in a Ford pickup truck, blocking the officer's personal car; this sparked an argument, and the men physically attacked the officer, who was wearing civilian clothes. He pulled out his gun and shot two of them. ``It doesn't appear to be a robbery at this time," a Miami-Dade police spokesman said, ``just a fight."

New York, NY, 2011: Two men are facing charges in connection with a botched Brooklyn robbery that ended in gunfire and left a Metropolitan Transportation Authority police officer in the hospital.

New York, NY, 2011: An off-duty Triboro-Bridge and Tunnel officer was shot and wounded in a wild gunfight at a Brooklyn car stereo shop with a group of four armed thugs who tried to rob the place.

Houston, TX, 2011: An off-duty police officer shot and killed a man who appeared to be reaching for a gun at an apartment complex in northeast Houston. The HPD said he was not in uniform, but was wearing clothes that identified him as a police officer. He was working an extra job as security at the apartments when he noticed two men inside a vehicle parked in the parking lot who appeared to be engaged in drug activity. A handgun was found inside the car.

Sallisaw OK, 2011: Oklahoma State Bureau of Investigation agents say that Officer Wendell Hughes was shot while driving along Highway 64 in Sallisaw. The suspect was arrested by police shortly after the shooting.

Philadelphia, PA 2011: Police said two people were shot, one of them an off-duty officer, inside a busy University City movie theater. 12 gunshots were fired, during which the officer was struck in the shoulder. Police said a 20-year-old college student (innocent bystander) was hit in the left leg. Police said the off-duty Harrisburg Capitol officer who attempted to stop a box-office robbery.

New York, NY, 2011: An off-duty cop was shot after he foiled the robbery of a Brooklyn car repair shop Saturday night when he got into a wild shootout with the bandits, cops said. Anthony Pressly, a Bridge and Tunnel cop, was waiting for his car to be fixed when four thugs suddenly burst in the garage and announced a robbery, sources said. Pressly, who was armed, grabbed his handgun to stop the pack of thieves, sparking a gun battle that sent bullets flying inside the Bedford-Stuyvesant shop.

Cleveland, OH, 2011: An off-duty police officer shot and killed a man outside of an eastside bar. Witnesses say they saw the subject shooting at another man in front of the bar. They say the officer identified himself as a police officer, then the subject Jones turned toward him with his gun in his hand. The officer shot Jones three times.

Belfast, Ireland, 2011: A man was shot and killed by an off-duty police offer during a suspected robbery at a petrol station. The dead man was in his mid-20s and it's believed he was trying to rob the filling station with a knife.

It is impossible to second guess all of these officers, and I would not want to even if I could. All I can say is that these officers took action, but did not remain unharmed. Some of the officers may now wish that they had waited, called, or let on-duty officers who were equipped with vests, communications equipment, and better weapons, handle the situations. I firmly agree that cops are never off-duty, and that it is almost impossible for us to resist the desire to help our fellow human beings. You *can* attempt to help others while offr-duty, but *should* you?

In Florida, you can shoot to stop the imminent commission of a forcible felony. How do you know if what you are seeing is a rape or a date? You cannot shoot for sexual battery (no penetration) but you can shoot for rape (penetration). How do you know what is happening down there without sticking your face down there?

Again, I teach that you have to come out of the action with several things intact, *or you lose:*

- Mentally unharmed
- Physically unharmed
- Emotionally unharmed
- Financially unharmed
- Reputation unharmed
- Legally unharmed
- Family unharmed
- Department unharmed

When you call it in, and you should call it in before taking action if you can, and let them know you are a cop, and give your description. Tell the dispatcher to tell the officers not to shoot you.

Now if you are in a mall and terrorists decide to shoot up the place, you may not be able to call first. Remember that not only cops may shoot you thinking you are a bad guy, but civilians who may be legally (or illegally) carrying may think you are one of the terrorists, and shoot you too. You must realize that being shot and killed does not help the innocent victims.

I firmly believe that we will see an uptick in the following types of attacks:

✓ Mass shootings or bombings at schools
✓ Mass shootings or bombings at work
✓ Mass shootings or bombings at church
✓ Mass shootings or bombings at malls
✓ Mass shootings or bombings at tourist attractions
✓ Mass shootings or bombings at outdoor cafés.

I firmly believe that we will see an uptick in the following types of armed robberies:

- ✓ Armed robberies at banks
- ✓ Armed robberies at convenience businesses
- ✓ Armed robberies at stores
- ✓ Armed robberies at fast food restaurants
- ✓ Armed robberies at stores

Before entering one of these places, do a tactical assessment. Think about what you would do if someone started to shoot, or someone tried to rob the place. Talk to your husband wife in advance, and tell them what you want them to do. Have a plan.

Let the spouse know that if you are wounded, coming to your aid only draws attention to you, makes it more likely that the shooter will try to shoot you again, or shoot your spouse. Coming to your aid brings you no comfort, does not help, and makes it more likely that you or your spouse will be killed, and that is not helpful.

Have a plan for what you would do if the shooter takes your spouse hostage. I believe that this hostage will be shot in most circumstances. If you are pointing a gun at the shooter, and the shooter is pointing a gun at you, then the shooter should be taking the shot.

To tip the scale in your favor, plan ahead. A good idea is to glance down with your eyes, signifying that the hostage should drop like a sack of oats. The shooter cannot hold them up, and this opens up the target for a quick multiple shot. The odds are that the shooter will focus attention on you and away from the spouse.

Your action time will beat the shooter's reaction time. I don't guarantee that you will win or your spouse will go unharmed, but I guarantee that a lack of a plan will make it more likely you or your spouse will die.

Finally, when uniformed police arrive, immediately put the gun down and let them cuff you up. You can try to yell "police", but don't count on the fact they know you. They might even think you are a cop who went crazy. There will be plenty of time to explain of you are not killed by responding uniformed officers.

If you have time, re-holster before uniformed police arrive, if it is safe to do so (shooter dead, or shooter cuffed). There is now a sash with "police" on it you can throw over your body to ID yourself. It looks goofy, but may save your life. It compacts into a tiny ball for storage in your bag.

Color Codes for
Combat Readiness

Jeff Cooper was a Marine Lieutenant Colonel who served in both World War II and the Korean War. Cooper was well known as a gun writer. Some of Cooper's thoughts and meditations were printed in gun magazines as "Cooper's Corner".

In the 1960s he coined the term hoplophobia, an irrational fear of weapons. One contribution to the firearms world was the "code system". This is sometimes called "Combat Mindset - The Cooper Color Code", published the book *Principles of Personal Defense* with Louis Awerbuck.

Cooper used color codes to describe levels of combat readiness. These levels represent awareness and the ability to deal with threats; the codes range from Condition White, where one is totally oblivious to surroundings, to Condition Red, where one is fighting for life. These color codes are listed here:

Code White Or Condition White: the person is unaware of what's going on. You are distracted, tired, or concerned about something else. Your judgment may be impaired by alcohol or drugs. The person in code white is unaware and unprepared.

If someone is attacked while in Condition White, only a random act, such as police arriving or a stranger interfering, or the lack of skill of the attacker will help the victim. The would-be victim may not believe that this is happening, may be in denial, and may not even be able to describe the attacker.

Code Yellow or Condition Yellow: You are aware and alert but calm and relaxed, scanning your surroundings for threats. You know who's in front of you, to your sides, and behind you. You don't think anyone will attack, but you are mentally ready in case something happens.

You are armed with some type of tool that will help you if you are in trouble, and in most conditions, that means armed with a full-sized battle pistol of appropriate caliber and capacity.

There is no specific threat in this situation. Your mindset is simply "I may have to defend myself, and today may be the day." A police officer would tell you that the world is sometimes a dangerous place populated by some unfriendly people, and you must be prepared to defend yourself, when necessary.

Whenever you are armed you should be in Condition Yellow. In unfamiliar neighborhoods, Condition Yellow is a must. You can remain in Yellow for long periods without much fatigue. In Condition Yellow, you are monitoring the areas in front of you, to the sides, and behind you. You should be aware of someone suddenly crossing the street for no apparent reason, in order to cross paths with yours.

Code Orange or Condition Orange: You sense that something is not right, and that you might be attacked. It is your "sixth sense" that is alerted. This is not "extrasensory perception", this is heightened-sensory perception that triggers long-buried instincts that tell your subconscious there is danger.

Police officers while on duty must be in Condition Orange. Your job as an officer is to notice a number of suspicious men standing around possibly dealing drugs instead of working in the middle of a weekday, or a man wearing a long coat comes on a summer's day. Remaining in Condition Orange is stressful and difficult for long periods of time.

In Condition Orange, you are aware of the positions of all potentially dangerous people around you, and any weapons they may be able to use, such as weapons of opportunity.

You may develop a mental plan for dealing with threats, and may have identified an egress route. Running away is always an option. Legally, financially, and physically, it is better not to be in a gunfight. You will not win any awards or the admiration of your friends, if your Sunday morning story is that you ran away from a mugger or a robber.

Being sued, being arrested, being interrogated, and being wounded are not fun, and your friends will soon forget your exciting story. Paying thousands of hard-earned dollars to an attorney is not exciting either.

This is a specific alert. In Condition Orange, react to an "if-then" statement; "If that person does something or makes an overt action to attack me, then I will be forced to do something to counteract it." If you are carrying a pistol, it is still holstered, but mentally you are thinking and rehearsing your draw and audible commands.

Use loud verbal commands that sound good to bystanders: "Leave me alone!" "If you don't stop attacking me I will shoot you." "Please don't move." "Police officer, let me see your hands!" "Drop the weapon"! "Back off!" "No se mueva! Suelte la barra!" (*Don't move! Drop the crowbar!*) "Volteese! Suelte la navaja!" (*Turn around! Drop the razor!*) Remember: only identify yourself as a police officer if you are a police officer. If you are, then make sure everyone knows it.

Some have advocated yelling "Please don't move!" The reason behind that, is that maybe someone will think you are saying "Police, don't move!" which may give them pause. I personally do not advocate this, since many offenders are shooting police officers these days, and a police officer, stat attorney, district attorney, or judge may not like the idea of a false personation of a police officer, even if you explain that you are just a polite individual.

Code Red or Condition Red: this is a battle posture. You only remain in this condition for a few minutes at a time. When someone is attacking you, you are reacting to the attack and defending yourself. Immediate action is necessary to stop your attacker, leave the area, and get help.

In this stage, you put your plan into action. You draw your pistol, give commands if there is time, and if the threat does not cease immediately, and if you are in fear for your life, and if not firing will likely result in great bodily harm or serious injury, you fire for center mass, and do not stop firing until the threat ceases.

Great bodily harm or serious injury means sever bleeding, broken bones, gunshot or knife wounds, blunt force trauma, or other injuries that are life-threatening.

Jeff Cooper wrote several books recounting his philosophies and life's adventures plus essays and short stories, including *To Ride, Shoot Straight and Speak the Truth.* Although Cooper and I disagree on gun choice (Cooper was a life-long fan of the Colt 1911, and I am an advocate for the Glock 22 or 35), I think that Cooper's books are valuable reading and highly recommended.

Carrying Gear While
Off-Duty

I really do have to recommend that if you carry a gun, you carry an extra magazine. I also have to recommend that if you carry a gun, you carry a badge. I also have to recommend that if you carry a badge, you have it in a holder that allows you to clip it to your belt or hang it around your neck. I further have to recommend that if you carry a gun, you carry handcuffs.

The handcuffs are something most of us won't carry. But think of this: what if you announce yourself and the shooter gives up? You can't just execute the shooter. You have to secure the shooter's weapon and the shooter; this is harder to do without handcuffs.

I also think the day of the cop badge wallet is over. What if you go to pay for gas and the guy behind you is waiting to rob the gas station. The robber looks over your shoulder and sees your "tin" as you get out your money. This guy will either: not rob the place (unlikely), or will take you out quickly then rob the place (likely).

Most cops use this type of wallet so they can "accidentally-on-purpose" expose the badge to an on-duty cop who has pulled them over in a traffic stop, so they can get out of a ticket the "cool-and-suave" way.

This is goofy. Put the badge in your lap or around your neck and forget subtlety. If you are going to badge your way out of a ticket, just do it. If the Trooper or Sheriff or whatever wants to let you off, he or she will just let you off. The badge wallet could get you killed in the store robbery scenario.

I wrote about this issue nearly 20 years ago, and cops are still using the old badge wallets. You can also see: Weissberg,

M. (1995): "Off Duty: Where is Your Badge?" *The Florida Trooper.* V. 10, No. 3. Fall. Pg. 43.

Things That Get
Us Killed

Bad tactics, bad equipment, lack of training, and other problems are not always the fault of the department. Here are the 10 Ten Deadly Errors of Law Enforcement and Police work, according to Brooks (1976) one more time. Read them as if your life depends on it!

1. LACK OF CONCENTRATION: If you fail to keep your mind on the job while on patrol or carry home problems into the field, you start to make errors. It can cost you and your fellow officers their lives.

2. TOMBSTONE COURAGE: Just what it says, if time allows wait for backup. There are very few instances where you should try and make a dangerous apprehension unaided.

3. NOT ENOUGH REST: To do your job you must be alert. Lack of sleep or being sleepy can endanger yourself, the community and fellow officers.

4. TAKING A BAD POSITION: Never let anyone you are questioning or about to stop get in a better position than you are. There is no such animal as a routine stop!

5. NOT HEEDING DANGER SIGNS: As a cop you will get to recognize "danger signs". Movements, strange cars, warnings that should alert you to watch your step and approach with caution. Know your beat and watch for what is out of place.

6. FAILURE TO WATCH THE HANDS OF A SUSPECT: Is he or she reaching for a weapon or getting ready to assault you? Where else can a potential killer strike from, but from their hands!

7. RELAXING TOO SOON: YES, the rut of false alarms, kids in the park after curfew, barking dog calls, traffic stops during daylight hours all become mundane in time. ALWAYS observe the activity. NEVER take any call as routine or just another false alarm. It could be your life on the line.

8. IMPROPER HANDCUFFING: Once you have made the arrest, handcuff the prisoner CORRECTLY! See that the hands that can kill you are safely secured.

9. NO SEARCH OR POOR SEARCH: There are too many places to hide a weapon that if you fail to search you are guilty of committing a crime against other officers that will have contact with your prisoner. Many people carry weapons and are able and ready to use them on you. Never assume that the next guy or the jailer will do a "good" search.

10. DIRTY OR INOPERATIVE WEAPON: Is your sidearm clean? How about the bullets? Did you clean your weapon since the last range day? Or have you even shot or practiced drawing your weapon recently? Can you hit your target in a combat situation? You must practice faithfully and religiously!

Brooks (1976) wrote *Officer Down, Code Three*. This is where this list originated from. The book is worth the money. According to Brooks' website, after a twenty year career, Pierce

Brooks retired as a captain with the reputation as one of the best detectives in the United States.

From time to time during Sergeant Friday's opening monologue on Dragnet, he announced the shift's Watch Commander as Lieutenant Pierce Brooks." After the Los Angeles Police Department, in May 1970, Chief Brooks served as the Director of Public Safety in Lakewood, Colorado. Brooks gained famed as the detective in Joseph Wambaugh's book, *The Onion Field.*

In case you want to read more about Pierce Brooks, the website is:

 http://www.policewriters.com/pierce_brooks.html

Glossary of
Holster Terms

Although a glossary often comes at the end of a book, I have included the glossary of gun terms here so that the reader will understand all terminology that is used in the section.

Adjustable rake: The angle which can be changed by the user.

Andrews Wait: A term popularized by police in Florida, to describe the wait time for a Sam Andrews Holster, a high quality holster that is made individually, and its popularity results in its taking a long time to get.

Ankle Holster: A holster specifically designed to worn on the ankle.

Appendix carry: A carry position where the holstered gun is placed forward of the hip on the strong side, between navel and the hip bone.

Askins Design: the Border Patrol style holster designed by legendary US Border Patrol firearms instructor Charles Askins. This holster had the rear cant but was made for the uniform Sam Browne belt.

Ballistic Nylon: A synthetic nylon fabric used for a variety of holster and pouch applications. Ballistic nylon was developed by the DuPont corporation for flak jackets to be worn by World War II airmen.

Behind the hip: A carry position where the holster is placed just behind the hip.

Bellyband: The bellyband allows concealed carry of multiple weapons and accessories around the midsection, in a variety of configurations.

Between pants & belt: A carry position where the holster is placed outside the pants, but inside the belt; favored by the author for wearing with a business shirt without the shirt becoming untucked.

Bianchi Style: An artificial holster material, such as Cordura or ballistic nylon. Monrovia Police Department Officer John Bianchi made holsters at night to sell to fellow cops. Fifty years later, Bianchi has sold over 40 million holsters. Bianchi history includes revolutionary holster design in ballistic weave nylon and other high-performance man-made materials. Due to the popularity of the Bianchi Ranger and Bianchi Accumold holsters, nylon and Cordura holsters are commonly known as Bianchi Holsters. The company is now owned by Safariland.

Body guard or sweat guard: See bodyshield.

Bodyshield: A term used to describe a shield that serves as a protective barrier between the weapon and shooter's body. Rumor has it Sam Andrews made the first ones.

Boning: A hand or machine process that adds detail shaping to the holster and shows the exact outline of the gun, the boning is done using a dummy gun made of pot metal.

Cant: The rake or angle. A straight cant and a forward cant are the most popular.

Carjacker: A Sam Andrews design, that was designed for use when seated in a vehicle or at a desk; it provides immediate access to the weapon. The loop-around flap slips beneath the belt's lower edge and comes up to snap to the holster back, folding over the top for a close and secure carry. This extreme cross draw mounts the holster in a horizontal method.

Chicago Screw: Screws commonly used for tension or retention in holsters. A male portion is normally slotted, and a female part accepts the male part. Stainless Chicago Screws, Aluminum Chicago Screws, Plastic Chicago Screws, and Brass Chicago Screws are common.

Clip or belt clip: A metal clamp, often covered with leather, which fits over the top half of the belt; commonly used in inside the pants or clip-on holsters.

Combination holster: A holster that can be worn either inside or outside both pants and belt.

Combination Kydex / leather: A holster which is made of both Kydex and leather.

Cordura: Cordura is a synthetic nylon fabric used for a variety of holster and pouch applications. The fabric was originally developed by DuPont in 1929 as a type of Rayon developed by E.I. du Pont de Nemours and Company. The product was further developed during World War II and used by the military in tires.

Covered trigger guard: A holster which completely covers the entire trigger area, so it is not possible to reach a finger in to touch the trigger of the holstered gun.

Cross draw: A holster that rides on the weak side, but the drawing motion is performed across the body with the shooting hand.

Custom holster: A holster that is made to the owner's specifications.

Drop: A lower position where the gun is held below the belt line. This is often more popular with motor officers for on-duty.

Extreme rake: A forward cant, but the muzzle will be angled more sharply forward.

FBI Cant: A forward cant, but the angle varies one holster manufacturer to another.

High ride or high rise: A higher position where the gun is held above the belt line.

Hook or J hook: A plastic or metal piece which partially encircles or hooks the belt, to keep the holster from coming out of the inside of the pants.

Injection-Molded: A process used to form Kydex or plastic holsters inside a mold by injecting melted polymer into the mold.

Inside the Pants: The holster is worn inside the waistband, and is placed inside both the pants and inside the belt.

Jordan Design: US Border Patrol Agent Bill Jordan designed a holster that was the chief design for police duty holsters for almost thirty years. The design exposed the trigger guard of the revolver. A wedge tilted the grip away from the body for rapid draw. It had a steel insert and tunnel belt loop.

Kydex: A polymer which is for rigid holsters. This thermoplastic material is used for a number of applications, including holsters, magazine carriers, handcuff carriers, and flashlight carriers.

Leather: Gun holster leather is usually made of cowhide or horsehide, but may be trimmed with exotic leathers such as shark or snakeskin. Leather is used for making holsters, magazine carriers, handcuff carriers, and flashlight carriers.

Level I retention: A holster with one retention device employed in the design; a simple thumb-break device that must be unsnapped in order to draw the weapon.

Level II retention: A holster with two retention devices employed in the design; a thumb-break is released then the pistol must be rocked forward or rearwards in the holster to clear some form of internal locking device before it can be drawn.

Level III retention: A holster with three retention devices employed in the design; both internal and external devices must be released.

Lined: Material on the inside of the holster, where the gun rides; occasionally refers to material on the back of the holster, where it touches your body.

Loop: A piece of a holster which completely encircles the belt.

M12: The Bianchi Model M12 Universal Military Holster designed by John Bianchi in the 1980's and known as the M12, the standard issue holster for the U.S. Armed Forces. The ambidextrous design, when combined with modular accessories, allows the M12 to be worn in 14 different positions.

Mangerie: (Pronounced like lingerie). A term coined by the author, and used to describe the elaborate fancy gunleather using animal skins, designed by Sam Andrews and worn by legendary MDPD DUI cop and police firearms instructor Jerry Davenport; the term means "Lingerie for men".

Military holster: A leather or Cordura holster with a flap covering the pistol.

Muzzle forward: The holstered gun will have its muzzle canted toward the front of your body.

Muzzle rear: The holstered gun will have its muzzle canted toward the rear.

Non-injection-molded: A process used where holsters are made by placing sheets of Kydex or plastic over a form and partially melting them until they conform to the desired shape.

Notebook Holster: An original Sam Andrews design, which incorporates a loose-leaf notebook, magazine holder, and holster in one. The gun is always concealed within a square cavern, covered by a Velcro-secured flap. The gun is retained in a scabbard that is boned to the shape of the individual gun.

Offset: The top part of the holstered gun is held away from the body by either using a wedge, or by the shape of the holster. Holsters which use both offset and drop are comfortable and used for duty gear.

Offside: The weak or non-shooting hand.

One-handed re-holstering: The holster will stay open without collapsing when the gun is drawn, enabling you to reholster without holding the holster open.

Open top: Holsters that do not have a retention strap.

Outside the Waistband: The holster is worn on the outside of the waistband.

Sam Browne Belt: a wide belt, 2.5 – 3 inches in width, made of leather, which sometimes has a cross strap diagonally over the shoulder. It is most often used for military or police uniform duty. Sam Browne was a British army officer serving in India in the 19th century. During the Rebellion of 1857 in India, Captain Sam Browne was serving with the 2nd Punjab Irregular Cavalry. Browne charged cannon and was attacked by one of its crew; Browne received a sword cut which severed his left arm at the shoulder. With no left hand, he found that he was unable to draw his sword, so he invented the cross strap.

Small of back: The holster is placed in the center of the back. Many manufacturers will not make this anymore, after lawsuits from wearers who were injured when the fell backwards and received spinal injuries from the gun hitting their bodies.

Paddle: A holster designed to be held onto the belt by a wide piece of leather or plastic.

Pancake: A holster with slotted wings on either side to hold on the belt which increase stability. Some holsters have three slots to give a choice of cant.

Plastic: A polymer which is less expensive and generally less sturdy than Kydex.

Rake: The angle at which the holster will hold the gun; the cant. It is measured by degrees.

Retention holster: A holster which has a security strap intended to prevent the gun from being drawn by anyone but the person wearing it.

Scabbard: A design which encloses the muzzle end.

Shooting Hand: The strong hand or dominant hand that the shooter naturally prefers to shoot with.

Shoulder holster: A holster that incorporates a harness worn over the shoulder or shoulders. The holster portion of this rig usually rides under the armpit of the wearers weak side.

Sight Track: A molded or formed tunnel in a holster that allows for the front sight.

Slide: Designs which do not enclose the muzzle end, allowing them to carry otherwise identical guns with different muzzle lengths.

Slot: An opening in the holster body or wing.

Small of the Back or SOB: Refers to a holster that carried in the small of the back near the spine.

Stability: How much the holster moves around when the wearer draws or re-holsters the gun.

Steel Hardtop: A band of steel which prevents the collapse of the holster top when the weapon is drawn.

Straight drop: The holstered gun will have its muzzle pointed straight toward the floor.

Strong Hand: The shooting hand or dominant hand that the shooter naturally prefers to shoot with.

Strong Side: A term used to describe the shooting hand side of the body; the side corresponding to the dominant hand.

Tactical Thigh Holster: Refers to a holster that worn on the thigh of the shooting hand side.

Tanning: Tanning is the process of making leather, using tannin, an acidic chemical compound, using the animal's brain (brain tanning) using chromium in the form of chromium sulfate (mineral tanning) or using tanning from vegetable materials (vegetable tanning).

Tension: How tightly the gun or magazine is held in the holster, usually by means of a tension screw.

Tension Screw: Refers to a screw mounted within the holster that allows the shooter to adjust the draw tension. See also *Chicago screw*.

Threepersons Design: A type of holster designed by Tom Threepersons. Cherokee Tom Threepersons was a legendary lawman serving in San Antonio and El Paso, Texas during the early 20th Century. The design was a strong-side, high-ride, open top holster with a modest forward cant, and a long retention strap. Many have elaborate floral carving.

Thumb break: a strap that goes over the top of the holstered gun and is snapped in place for security. Called a thumb break because the thumb must break it open in order to draw the weapon. Some states mandate a thumb break holster.

Torque Plate: A spring steel reinforcement plate which creates a stiffened paddle over which the belt lays when the holster is worn.

"Tuckable" or shirt-tuck: A feature that enables a shirt to be tucked in over the holstered gun, leaving only the holster's loops or J-hooks visible on the belt line.

Tunnel: The belt is completely enclosed within the holster for some distance.

Weak Hand: The non-shooting hand or non-dominant hand that the shooter naturally does not prefer to shoot with.

Weak Side: A term used to describe the non-shooting hand side of the body; the side corresponding to the non-dominant hand.

Weissberg Shock and Awe Holster: A shoulder holster designed by the author and made by Sam Andrews that places the handgun under the left arm, and the TASER and a spare handgun magazine under the right arm, in the case of a right-handed shooter. This allows plain-clothes detectives or off-duty cops to carry an X26 TASER.

Weissberg TASER Holster: A carjacker type holster designed by the author and made by Sam Andrews. This allows plain-clothes detectives or off-duty cops to carry an X26 TASER cross draw, as most departments, and TASER International mandate.

Wet Molding: A type of boning normally done on wet leather soaked in lukewarm water.

Holsters

Holsters can be made of leather, plastic, Kydex, Cordura, cloth, wood, or even string. There are hundreds of manufacturers that make holsters one at a time, or hundreds each day. A holster can be had for as little as five dollars. I have seen holsters costing over five hundred dollars.

A newer trend is for some makers to produce holsters made of exotic skins. Alligator, Crocodile, Ostrich, Frog, Shark, Elephant, Deerhide, Moose, Hippopotamus, Stingray, Tegu Lizard, Monitor Lizard, Python, Buffalo, Horsehide, and Rhinoceros are all being used now to make holsters. The term "Mangerie" was coined by the author, and used to describe the elaborate fancy Sam Andrews gunleather worn by DUI cop and police firearms instructor Jerry Davenport. Davenport, an African big game hunter, favored elephant hide. "Mangerie" means "Lingerie for men".

One of the simplest holsters ever made is the "string holster" or "loop holster" used by the OSS in World War II. Using a string or leather thong, make a circle or loop. One end of the loop is tucked under the belt. Then there are two loops both of which are tucked inside the pants, similar to IWB. Your handgun is then put inside the pants through the two loops.

The idea behind this carry method is to provide some retention, yet still be able to get rid of the gun and not have to remove a holster from the belt. When gun is discarded, the wearer pulls on one end of the loop and the throws away the loop of string.

There are many types of holsters. There are photos in this

book of many types of holsters. Some are better designs than others. To review every type of holster would be impossible, but some of the pros and cons of the various types are presented here.

One must always remember that there are as many opinions as there are people; no one's opinion matters more than yours. You will have to lug this gun around. It makes sense to collect others' opinions like a child collecting fallen leaves. An opinion can be discarded easily without thought, just like that child can discard a leaf without remorse.

Just because a "gunwriter" or a police officer, or a firearms instructor recommends a particular type, style, or maker, does not mean you have to buy it. You can try several holsters and try them, keep your favorite, and sell the rejects on Ebay or at a gun show. Your reject will be someone else's perfect holster.

Remember that when you deal with a custom holster maker, their wares are produced one at a time. Some makers are backed up for weeks or months. Some makers do not answer their phones, have voice mail that does not accept messages, deal only with email or shopping carts on their websites, or have trouble returning messages. Be prepared to wait a long time, and pay big bucks for custom work, especially with custom skins.

In the contact section at the end of this book, there is a list of manufacturers. Some makers were impossible to get hold of. In some cases, there is a notation: *"NOTE: This maker did not participate in this book."* This does not necessarily mean that they refused to participate. Some makers could not provide holsters, or could not afford to provide holsters.

Holsters – Pros and Cons

Ankle Holster

A holster specifically designed to worn on the ankle. The ankle holster can be worn on the opposite or weak side with the butt to the rear, allowing the gun to be drawn across the body (diagonally), or on the strong side with the butt to the front, for a reverse draw, using a "left-handed" holster for a "right handed" shooter (Weissberg Draw).

Bellyband

The bellyband allows concealed carry of multiple weapons and accessories around the midsection, in a variety of configurations. This can be hot and constricting, and the draw can be difficult, and re-holstering almost impossible.

Belt Slide

The belt slide, with name such as the Galco Jac Slide, Galco, Milt Sparks, or DeSantis Yaqui Slide, and other designs, do not enclose the muzzle end, allowing them to carry otherwise identical guns with different muzzle lengths. The drawback is there is little or no retention, and little or no protection for the gun. The trigger guard is usually covered, and the holster may fit several different makers' guns.

Carjacker

A Sam Andrews design, that was designed for use when seated in a vehicle or at a desk; it provides immediate access to the weapon. The loop-around flap slips beneath the belt's lower edge and comes up to snap to the holster back, folding over the top for a close and secure carry. This extreme cross draw mounts the holster in a horizontal method. The carjacker is a great choice for women, who tend to be flat on the abdomen, as opposed to a pancake, which is not as good for women, who are curved on the sides.

Cross Draw

A holster that rides on the weak side, but the drawing motion is performed across the body with the shooting hand. The cross draw is a good choice for those sitting at a desk or in a car. The cross draw is a great choice for women, who tend to be flat on the abdomen, as opposed to a pancake, which is not as good for women, who are curved on the sides.

Inside the Pants

The holster is worn inside the waistband, and is placed inside both the pants and inside the belt. This can be uncomfortable for overweight men. If carried in appendix, this can be a good carry for women; on the hip strong side, this is not as good for women. Overweight men may not find the IWP appendix comfortable especially while seated.

ISPC Pancake

Renamed the IPSC Saddle Holster, this Andrews design combines the high, close carry of the pancake style with the ease and speed of draw found in competition holsters. The weapon is secured by a thumb break, and has spring steel reinforcement around cutaway front or modified around cutaway front. This style was copied by Bianchi, Don Hume and BlackHawk Leather. This style allows for a break front version of the Border Patrol Draw.

Notebook Holster

Surprise, another Sam Andrews nightmare. A nightmare for your assailant, that is. The obvious benefit to this design, is that the bystander or assailant will not know you are carrying. The drawback is that you can forget the whole thing on the restaurant table or leave it in the car. Uncle Mike's took this design and mass produced it in nylon Cordura.

Pancake

A pancake holster has slotted wings on either side to hold on the belt which increase stability. Some holsters have three slots to give a choice of cant. This holster acts like a saddle on a horse, molding to the wearer's hip. The pancake is a great choice for men, who tend to be curved on the abdomen, as opposed to a cross draw, which is not as good for men, who are curved on the front. Women wearing this worn on the hip may find this holster prints and makes this hard to conceal.

Small of the Back

The holster is placed in the center of the back. Many manufacturers will not make this anymore, after lawsuits from wearers who were injured when the fell backwards and received spinal injuries from the gun hitting their bodies.

Carrying the handgun at the small of the back offers good concealment, since the covering garment can fall open without revealing the holstered handgun. When the victim is being robbed, he can go to withdraw his wallet, and instead draw the gun.

The SOB is a great choice for women, who tend to be flat on the small of the back, as opposed to a pancake, which is not as good for women, who are curved on the sides. If a man or woman is overweight and has "love handles" that make the small of the back bulge, this can be uncomfortable.

Shoulder Holster

A holster that incorporates a harness worn over the shoulder or shoulders. The holster rides under the armpit of the wearer's weak side. This is a great solution for a detective or administrator who sits at a desk for most of the day; the odds are that the uniforms will make fun of you and call you "Don Johnson" or "Sonny Crockett". If you are an administrator, you can make the uniforms write memos for being insubordinate.

Weissberg Shock and Awe

A holster that incorporates a harness worn over the shoulders. The primary firearm holster rides under the armpit of the wearer's weak side. The TASER holster rides under the armpit of the wearer's strong side, along with a spare magazine for the primary weapon.

This is a solution for a detective or administrator who sits at a desk for most of the day, but wants to have access to a less-lethal solution, without having to rely on deadly force in situations that may not warrant it; the odds are that the uniforms will make fun of you; in my case, I ask them what they invented this week. A Sam Andrews exclusive, designed by the author.

Weissberg Cross draw TASER Holster

A holster that rides on the weak side, but the drawing motion is performed across the body with the shooting hand. The cross draw is mandated for TASER carry. The loop-around flap slips beneath the belt's lower edge and comes up to snap to the holster back, folding over the top for a close and secure carry.

This cross draw mounts the holster in a more horizontal method. The carjacker is a great choice for women, who tend to be flat on the abdomen, as opposed to a pancake, which is not as good for women, who are curved on the sides; a Sam Andrews exclusive, designed by the author.

Knives
Glossary of Knife Terms

Once again, although a glossary often comes at the end of a book, I have included the glossary of knife terms here so that the reader will understand all terminology that is used in the section.

Abaniko: a fixed blade knife designed by Bram Frank.

Alloy: a steel that combines two or more elements. A combination of carbon, chromium, manganese, molybdenum, nickel, and vanadium.

Automatic knife: sometimes called a switchblade, the knife opens with the touch of a button, via a spring assist. Some federal and local laws regulate the ownership or sale of these knives; the best known are made by Benchmade.

Balisong: a Filipino adaptation of a Spanish sailor's knife that is sometimes called a "butterfly knife".

Bushido: three Japanese words which when combined mean "the way of the warrior-student".

Common pocket knife: A folding knife usually with a blade or 4" or less. This is a legal term in some states.

CRKT: Columbia River Knife & Tool

CRIMPT: Close Range Medium Impact Tool, designed by Bram Frank.

Dagger: a short, thick, double-edged blade, commonly carried in a boot or on a belt.

Damascus blade: two or more different colors of steel are folded together and forged to create patterns of color. A strong, sharp, visually pleasing blade with a natural camouflage is the result.

Desangut: a kinetic opening knife designed by Bram Frank, based on a Filipino Kerambit knife.

Drop Forged: When heated metal is hammered into the recesses of a die.

Drone: a training knife made of metal.

Edge: The part of the blade that does the cutting.

Fixed Blade: a knife that does not fold.

Folder: A knife that folds; a common pocket knife, usually with a blade or 4" or less; the most famous historically are made by Buck Knives.

Forward Hammer Grip: one holds the knife upright, blade coming out the top of the gripping hand, as one would grab a hammer.

Full Tang: when the tang of a fixed bladed knife goes all the way through the handle portion to the end.

Grandmaster: usually a 7th degree black belt or higher rank, in any style.

Gunting: a kinetic opening knife designed by Bram Frank.

Hammer Forged: when layers of steel are folded and pounded together for strength and flexibility. Samurai Katanas, and Wakazashis were made in this method. Some were folded 200 times or more.

Ice-pick grip: The *Reverse Grip* is also called the *ice-pick grip* because an ice pick is held in that manner. It is the same as a *Hammer Grip* except the blade comes out the bottom of the hand rather than the top.

Kerambit: a Filipino knife with a ring on one end.

Kinetic Opening: Using the ramp on a Gunting-style folding knife to open the knife on your own body part or an opponent's.

Lapu-Lapu Corto: a kinetic opening knife designed by Bram Frank.

Persian Butt: when the butt of the knife has a Persian style end which gives a pinky hold to the handle and the rounded Persian end also allows for maximum transference of energy in a hammer fist strike. Percussive striking with the butt cap is enhanced with a round end rather than a flat or sharply pointed end cap.

Pocket Clip: a metal or plastic clip that allows a folder to be carried in a pocket, but does not allow it to slip inside the pocket.

Professor: the acknowledged highest ranking instructor in a style. The professor may be the founder of a style, or may have inherited the title. A Professor normally has a 10th degree black belt or higher (some styles have 11 or 12 ranks).

Quillion: a hand guard that keeps the hand from sliding down on the blade, and guards the hand from an opponents knife; usually found on fixed blade knives.

Ramp: a part on the back of the blade of a Gunting-style folding knife to open the knife used to open the knife on your own body part or an opponents; also used to deliver a hammer or tomahawk strike.

Reverse Grip:
The common name of the *Reverse Grip* is the *ice-pick grip* because an ice pick is held in that manner. It is the same as a *Hammer Grip* except the blade comes out the bottom of the hand rather than the top.

Rockwell: a scale for determining hardness of a blade.

Saber Grip: One holds the knife upright, blade coming out the top of the gripping hand, as one would grab a hammer. The difference between the *Hammer Grip* and the *Saber Grip* is the placement of the thumb and the actual use of the knife while in the different grips.

Sensei: a teacher, in any style.

Sifu: a teacher, in any style.

Siko: a kinetic opening knife designed by Bram Frank, made by Mantis Knives.

Spetznatz knife: a knife where the blade is spring loaded and shoots out of the handle as a projectile, a distance of 20-30 feet. This type of knife is illegal to own in many states.

Steel: in knife-making, refers to 440C, Damascus, ATS-34, 420, carbon, and other steels.

Stiletto: a long, thin, springy blade.

Tanto Blade: a Japanese style blade that has a chisel point for strength.

Thumb Hole: A hole in the blade that allows the blade to be opened one-handed; the best known round models are made by Benchmade and Spyderco. The triangular style was designed by Bram Frank.

Trainer: a training knife made of resin or metal.

Tusok: a kinetic opening knife designed by Bram Frank.

Z'mora: a kinetic opening knife designed by Bram Frank, made by Mantis Knives.

Note: I am sure you noticed the name Bram Frank mentioned here several times. Since Bram taught me most of what I know about knives, I have included some terms that Bram invented. I use these terms, because I think that all cops who carry knives should be familiar with knives, and should train to use knives.

Knives and the Police

A knife is a cutting tool. A knife separates one thing from another. The knife is one of the oldest and most useful tools ever invented by man. The first stone knives were broken, pressure flaked, or knapped. Early stone breakers simple hammers made of stone, wood, or antler to shape stone tools.

The Native Americans relied on stone, flint, chert, or obsidian knives for centuries. Obsidian knives are so sharp, and retain their edge so well, that they are used in surgery; they are many times sharper than surgical steel scalpels.

Police officers use their knives as prybars, general purpose tools, box cutters, letter openers, rescue tools, and in extreme cases, weapons of last resort.

The police officer has many tools on the gunbelt that are approved and manufacturer for police work. The handgun, TASER, baton, handcuffs, radio, and magazines can all be used as defensive or offense tools, and can be used to save the life of the officer.

A folding knife, kept in the front or rear pocket, gun side (strong side) or offside (weak side) can be used to save the life of the officer, when the officer is down on the ground, being straddled or stomped, especially when the officer is lying on the gun. Some cops carry two knives, so that one is accessible no matter which side the officer is lying on.

The knife can be deployed and used to poke, cut, slash,

slice, or lever the offender off the officer. The knife can be used as a pressure point striking device, to trap fingers or grab flesh, or to block.

There is no way I would attempt to distill down years of training with knives in a book. I believe in reading books about this, but it is not possible to substitute a book about knives for live training.

The practitioners of Filipino knife fighting are the best in the world, in my humble opinion. There are many "knife cultures" in the world.

Mexicans, Nicaraguans, Cubans, Spaniards, Guatemalans, Brazilians, and Argentineans, have all developed amazing knife cultures. The Chinese, Japanese, Thai, Indonesians, Koreans, and Indians had unbelievable knife cultures, whose popularity has waned in later years. But today, no culture can match the Filipinos for modern knife fighting, and that is because of one man: Remy Amador Presas.

Most cops are allowed to carry a knife. Most departments' General Orders, Standard Operating Procedures, or Departmental Orders, have little or no commentary on the style, design, blade length, or type of knife that an office may carry. Most police administrators know little about knives. Mark Overton, retired Chief of Police of Hialeah, Florida, and current Assistant Chief of Miami Beach, Florida, is an exception.

Knife Grips

The knife is an interesting tool, and the blades, carry methods, and even grips vary wildly. I will recommend you read Conceptual Modern Arnis by Grandmaster
Bram Frank for a full accounting, but I will mention that the forward or hammer grip, the saber grip, and the reverse or "ice pick" grip, the Filipino or "cancer grip", and the fencing grip are the most common grips.

Some would say that the only way you can tell if someone is a trained knife fighter is that they hold the knife in a reverse grip. Remy Presas, possibly the world's foremost expert on the blade, would say that this grip shortens your range, and that a forward grip gives more reach.

How much more can I write about knife grips? Instead, I got world-renown knife Grandmaster Bram Frank to demonstrate the following grips for you:

- The forward or "hammer grip"
- The reverse or "ice pick grip"
- The Filipino or "cancer grip"
- The "fencing grip"
- The "saber grip"

The forward or "hammer" grip
Demonstrated by Grandmaster Frank
In Photo Gallery at the end of the book
(Photo used by permission of Bram Frank)

The reverse or "ice pick" grip
Demonstrated by Grandmaster Frank
In Photo Gallery at the end of the book
(Photo used by permission of Bram Frank)

The Filipino or "cancer grip"
Demonstrated by Grandmaster Frank
In Photo Gallery at the end of the book
(Photo used by permission of Bram Frank)

The "fencing grip"
Demonstrated by Grandmaster Frank
In Photo Gallery at the end of the book
(Photo used by permission of Bram Frank)

The "saber grip"
Demonstrated by Grandmaster Frank
In Photo Gallery at the end of the book
(Photo used by permission of Bram Frank)

Knife Carry

Certainly the debate rages about carrying a folder upside-down, in the front or back pocket, on the off side or the strong side, or to carry one, two, or three knives.

You can buy holsters or sheaths made of thin sheets of plastic or polymer, leather, nylon, cordura, or other materials. There are neck sheaths, and pouches, and belts with sheaths built in.

The boot dagger will never go out of style; someone will always be able to sell a Sykes-Fairbain-Applegate dagger, and the "CIA delta dart" and the new glass-filled or plastic daggers are certainly popular with kids and the *Soldier of Fortune* reader.

Sam Andrews will be happy to build you a holster that allows you to carry a fixed blade, although most departments would frown at you. Sam's first thought is to build something cool that the customer would love; it's up to the departments to catch up to his vision.

I have to take this opportunity to mention that no reasonable person takes a knife to a gunfight. I will also mention that if you take a knife to a knife fight, you will get cut and injured. You will violate the rule that you must go home unharmed; you will be ignoring the rule that steel cuts flesh. If you bring a knife to a fistfight, you have a better chance.

A knife is a tool, nothing more; if you stay home and don't

go to the fistfight, knife fight, or gunfight, you are in the best position of all.

Blunt Weapons and Weapons of Opportunity

The Cold Steel Pocket Shark is an interesting offering from Lynn C. Thompson. I knew Lynn way back, and he is a true genius at marketing, and also at identifying weapons from other cultures, and turning things into weapons of opportunity.

According to Cold Steel's marketing, "Superficially, it shares many features common to most markers, but appearances can be deceptive. For starters, it's made from high impact plastic and features walls that are 4 times thicker than similar markers. This means it's built for impact and will survive the meanest blows and roughest treatment imaginable and still function like new. Plus, the screw on cap will stay in place and won't pop off like a regular marker's cap and leak all over your clothes." At $6.99 retail, it costs about what a Sharpie marker costs.

Another offering from cold steel is the Koga. The Koga is a *yawara* type stick, which could really be replaced with a length of closet rod or a plastic bar available at a hardware store. A gunsmith's Babbit bar would do also.

Bob Koga, a Jiu Jitsu, Judo and Aikido practitioner, was an LAPD cop for 25 years. This device is best used utilizing the Professor Wally Jay "Small Circle Jiu-Jitsu" techniques, or the pressure points popularized by Professor George Dillman. The item is made of it is injection molded from super tough black polypropylene.

Cold Steel's marketing states "blows struck with the fist may be too weak, or worse, result in a broken hand, while blows struck with a baton may be too powerful resulting in grave injury or even death. The SD however, solves this problem, neatly bridging the gap by concentrating and magnifying the effect of hand blows while minimizing the likelihood of permanent injury or death."

I have to say that anything can be deadly, including empty hand. Wally Jay beat on me for awhile in the 1990's, and if he tossed you around, you would agree. Wally died at age 94, born in 1917 and was still active to the end. The Koga SD1 retails for $11.99 and the Koga SD1 retails for $9.99.

Pens, ranging from Mont Blanc Le Grand at $400, through a Sharpie marker at $3 can be used defensively. I like a Sharpie. I took my wife Erika to New Orleans recently, and took a Sharpie with me on the plane. The Sharpie is plastic, writes as a marker, needs no excuse, and can be used as a *yawara*.

The *yawara*, also called a *pasak* or a *dulodulo* in Filipino martial arts, is a weapon used in various martial arts. The *yawara* originated from the use of a Buddhist object, by monks during Feudal Japan. The *yawara* is a small, thick stick which sticks out about an inch from each side of the hand. *yawara* are used for pressure point strikes.

The stick, whether Koga, *yawara*, pen, or whatever, is a last ditch tool, or tool that can be safely and legally carried when knives or firearms are prohibited.

I am frustrated and annoyed that the idiots that run things will not let certified, qualified police officers, who carry, train with, and work with guns, carry those guns on a plane or in an airport. When I was a federal agent, I was able to carry on a plane. As a Police Sergeant and police firearms instructor, who has passed a polygraph, background check, psychological, and training program, I was not allowed to carry.

A pilot, who probably would not pass the background to

be a cop, can, however, fly the plane into a building, say for instance, the Pentagon or World Trade Center, and not have to go through an equivalent polygraph, background check, and psychological.

But I can practice, train with, and carry a marker. In other instances, I can carry a "tactical pen", such as those made by Smith and Wesson, Uzi, Schrade, or Benchmade. These pens can be used as *yawara*, or to dig into pressure points, gouge eyes, joint locks, or for pain compliance.

-

Safety
Bill Jordan's Lesson

The late legendary Bill Jordan For those of you who aren't familiar with him, Bill Jordan is best known as an old-school US Border Patrolman, proponent of fast-draw instinct or "point" shooting, and the designer (at least in part) of the Jordan grips and Jordan holster.

Jordan was one of the major voices calling for the Smith &Wesson Model 19 "Combat Magnum", and later the round that became the .41 Magnum. His lesser known feats are his time in the United States Marine Corps, serving in action as an officer during World War II and the Korean War. For ten years he was an instructor in the pistol and police shotgun combat shooting at the Camp Perry Nat'l Matches.

Jordan reportedly had a tragic accidental discharge at the Chula Vista Border Patrol station in 1956. A .357 Magnum revolver he was handling at the time discharged, and the bullet penetrated a partition wall, striking a fellow Border Patrol Inspector in the head, killing him.

It seem that a long-standing familiarity with firearms breeds complacency, and the more experienced shooters have to exercise greater caution to overcome it. He retired from his 30 year career in the Border Patrol in 1965 with the rank of Assistant Chief Patrol Inspector.

John A. Rector, Patrol Inspector
Date of Birth: August 23, 1898
Began at INS: March 13, 1928
Date Died: October 16, 1956

At approximately 11:30 a.m., October 16, 1956, Patrol Inspector John A. Rector was accidentally shot by the firing of a .357 Magnum revolver by a fellow officer. The mishap occurred at the Chula Vista Sector Headquarters where two officers were discussing various guns and their limitations and advantages.

During the course of the conversation, the .357 Magnum was unloaded, examined, then reloaded, and placed in a desk drawer. The two officers then examined a .22 revolver and soon the discussion returned to the .357 Magnum.

At this point one of the officers reached into the desk drawer, picked up the pistol, and without realizing that it had been reloaded, pulled the trigger.

The bullet passed through a partition wall into Patrol Inspector Rector's office where it struck him in the left jaw and ranged up through his head.

Upon arrival of an ambulance and a doctor, Patrol Inspector Rector was removed to the Paradise Valley Hospital in National City. Two neurosurgeons from San Diego were called; however, nothing could be done for Inspector Rector. He died at approximately 2:00 p.m. the same day."

Safety
Col. Jeff Cooper's Lesson

I introduced the late Legendary Jeff Cooper to you earlier in this book. Col. Cooper once destroyed an electric meter mounted on a pole outside his study window while dry-firing a revolver in the presence of a journalist.

Cooper , a retired Colonel, authored the color code system and wrote for gun magazines for years as the "Gunners Guru". I bet the Colonel never forgot the embarrassment he felt when he screwed up in front of the journalist. Could you?

Safety
Scott Spjut's Last Lesson

In the police business, we subscribe strongly to the Latin mantra *"De mortius nil nisi bonum"* meaning "Say nothing but good of the dead". Whenever an officer is killed, we never analyze the mistakes that the deceased officer might have made that could have been factors in the death. I hate that tradition. If there is something there that can save another officer's life, it is not an insult to the honored dead to learn from their mistakes, it is a tribute. I intend to violate this time honored code, to tell you about a great man, Scott Spjut.

West Valley City, Utah, Forensic Director Scott Spjut died January 2, 2003, shot by an SKS Rifle. Scott was a weapons expert, forensic investigator, and renowned instructor. He would have told you that the Samozariadnyia Karabina Simonova (SKS) Gas operated, Semi-automatic fire rifle which weighed (loaded) 8.8 lbs., had a barrel of 20.34 inches, and an overall length of 40.16 inches, fired a 7.62 x 39 Soviet M43 (Type PS ball) 122 gr. bullet at 2411 fps., and was good to 1000 meters. This is the rifle that killed Scott.

So how does a nationally renowned forensics expert accidentally get shot and killed in a crime lab? The rifle he was processing accidentally discharged and struck him in the chest.

Typically, most labs and departments mandate that all firearms are required to be unloaded before they are booked into evidence. But according to published news reports, "this particular investigation apparently required Spjut to process the weapon while it was loaded", said West Valley Assistant Chief Craig Gibson.

The 38-year old Scott Spjut had worked for five years for

the City, but had worked as a forensics investigator since 1991. He traveled extensively to train others in forensics techniques.

I never had the chance to learn from or teach with Scott Spjut. The last lesson that Instructor Scott Spjut will ever teach is that safety matters, even if you are a world renowned expert.

I teach firearms at the police academy and forensic firearms identification at the academy to crime scene investigators. Every time I teach, no matter if the student is a rookie who never before handled a gun, or a SWAT team leader, ex-marine Gunnery Sergeant who had killed in combat, I teach the gun safety rules. Every time, there is always one student who bitches about having to hear them again.

To Scott's friends, family, and co-workers, I make this vow: to teach his last lesson for him, over and over and over and over. You can never hear these safety rules enough times. You can never be too careful.

- Weissberg's rule #1 is: Dead is dead.
- Weissberg's rule #2 is: You can't change dead.
- Weissberg's rule #3 is: You can't change rule number one or rule number two.

My rules are harsh, but true. The National Rifle Association's Golden Rule of Safety is as simple as it is true: Always point the muzzle in a safe direction. The Florida Fish and Wildlife Conservation Commission, formerly known as the Florida Game and Freshwater Fish Commission, teaches thousands of students gun safety annually. I have been an instructor in this program, which includes live fire, for fourteen years now, and have taught over 10,000 students, and have never had an unintentional discharge on my range. Never.

The Florida Fish and Wildlife Conservation Commission teaches ten rules for gun safety. Here they are, in no order of importance:

- Watch the muzzle.
- Treat every gun with the respect due a loaded gun.
- Be sure the barrel and action are clear of obstructions.
- Be sure of your target before you pull the trigger.
- Unload guns when not in use.
- Never point a gun at anything that you do not want to shoot.
- Never climb, run, or jump with a loaded gun.
- Never shoot at a flat, hard surface, or at water.
- Store guns and ammunition separately.
- Avoid alcoholic beverages and prescription medicines before or during shooting.

Of course these rules can be modified for the lab or for the field, but in each and every firearms accident where someone is injured or killed, one or more of these rules were violated. There are no exceptions.

Ever notice how a dead person doesn't look quite "real"? They aren't animated. They don't wake up. They don't breathe, talk, or laugh. There is no capillary refill when you squeeze the hand. They don't kiss you back. They don't answer your questions. If this article saves just one life, then it will be worth violating that unspoken rule, that we don't assign blame to the dead for their mistakes.

Scott Spjut died doing what he loved. It is a great thing to die doing what you love. It is greater still to live doing what your tour of duty and live to suck up that pension for years, and years. Scott, I hope I did well teaching this, your last class.

I always wanted to take training with Scott. If any of Scott's family or friends read this book, do not take offense that I used his lesson to save the lives of other sons, brothers, fathers, and officers. Take the time to remember Scott, and realize that he is still teaching lessons, although in this, a different classroom.

This section of the book
dedicated to the memory of
Scott Russell Spjut
July 01, 1964 - January 02, 2003

Contacts

An incomplete list of the contact information for the companies featured in this book.

Aker International, Inc.
2248 Main Street Suite 6
Chula Vista, CA 91911
(619) 423-5182
http://www.akerleather.com/

Andrews Custom Leather
Sam Andrews
22610 NW 102nd Ave
Alachua, Fl 32615
(386) 462-0576

Accurate Plating and Weaponry, Inc.
Bob Cogan
5229 County Road 99
Newville, Alabama 36353
(334) 585-9488

Bell Charter Oak Holsters
(607) 783-2483
PO Box 198 Gilbertsville NY 13776

Bianchi
3120 E. Mission Blvd.
Ontario, CA 91761
(800) 347-1200
http://www.bianchi-intl.com/

Blade-Tech Industries
5530 184th St E
Suite A
Puyallup, WA 98375
(877) 331-5793
http://www.blade-tech.com/
NOTE: This maker did not participate in this book.

Bowen Knife Company
800-397-4794
http://www.bowenknife.com/

Brigade Gun Leather
33301 Osawatamie Rd.
Osawatamie, KS 66064
913-755-3139
http://www.brigadegunleather.com/index.html
NOTE: This maker did not participate in this book.

Coffman Concealment Concepts, LLC
Michael Coffman
mcoffman@coffmanconcealment.com
503-348-3699

CrossBreed Holsters
224 N Main
Republic MO 65738
888-732-5011
http://www.crossbreedholsters.com/

Crossfire Holsters
6523 Spring Meadow Dr,
West Palm Beach, FL 33413
(954) 242-0865
Crossfireholsters.com

Coronado Leather
1-800-283-9509
http://coronadoleather.com
NOTE: This maker did not participate in this book.

DeSantis Gunhide
DeSantis Holster & Leather Goods Co.
431 Bayview Avenue
Amityville, NY 11701
800-424-1236
http://www.desantisholster.com/

D.M. Bullard Leather Mfg.
1100 Arvel Circle
Azle, TX 76020-6035
(866) 383-6761
(817) 444-9456
http://www.dmbullardleather.com/
NOTE: This maker did not participate in this book.

Don Hume Leathergoods
A Division Of
Oklahoma Leather Products, Inc.
500 26th Street NW
Miami, OK 74354
(800) 331-2686
http://www.donhume.com/

Galco International
2019 West Quail Avenue
Phoenix, Arizona 85027
1(800) USGALCO
http://www.usgalco.com/

Galls, Inc.
Exclusive Supplier for
Gould and Goodrich Holster with Mag Carrier
800-477-7766
http://www.galls.com/

Glock, USA
770-432-1202
6000 Highlands Parkway
Smyrna, GA 30082
http://us.glock.com

Graham's Custom Gun Leather
This maker provides no contact information.
Contact is by email only.
graham_holsters@comcast.net
http://www.grahamholsters.com/
NOTE: This maker did not participate in this book

Grandmaster Bram Frank
http://www.cssdsc.com
http://www.bramfrankknives.com
arnisman@aol.com

Gould and Goodrich
709 E. McNeil St.
Lillington, NC 27546
(800) 277-0732
http://www.gouldusa.com/

Haugen Handgun Leather
PO Box 6124
Bismarck, ND 58506-6124
(701) 255-0723
gunlethr@bis.midco.nethttp://haugenhandgunleather.com/
holsters/pc/home.asp

Hellweg
Available through Brownells
(800) 741-0015
200 South Front Street
Montezuma, Iowa 50171
http://www.brownells.com/
http://www.hellweg.com.au/

J. Aker
K. Aker International, Inc.
2248 Main Street
Suite 6
Chula Vista, California 91911-3932
(619) 423-5182
http://www.akerleather.com/

K&D Holsters
P.O. Box 4192
Plant City, FL 33563
813-659-3456
www.kdholsters.com
NOTE: This maker did not participate in this book

Kramer Handgun Leather
P.O. Box 112154
Tacoma, WA 98411 USA
800-510-2666
http://www.kramerleather.com/

Mantis Knives Headquarters
1580 N. Harmony Circle
Anaheim, CA 92807
(714) 701-9136
http://www.mantisknives.com

Maxpedition
PO Box 5008
Palos Verdes, CA 90274
(877) 629-5556
http://www.maxpedition.com/
NOTE: This maker did not participate in this book.

Mernickle Custom Holsters
1875 View Court
Fernley, Nevada
89408
775-575-3166
www.mernickleholsters.com

Milt Sparks

605 E 44 St. #2

Boise, ID 83714

208-377-5577

http://www.miltsparks.com/

NOTE: This maker did not participate in this book.

Mitch Rosen

540 No. Commercial Street

Manchester, New Hampshire 03101

(603) 647-2971

http://www.mitchrosen.com/

NOTE: This maker did not participate in this book.

Safariland

13386 International Parkway

Jacksonville, FL 32218

Or

3120 East Mission Blvd.

Ontario, CA 91761

(800) 347-1200

http://www.safariland.com/

Sturm Ruger

411 Sunapee Street

Newport, NH 03773

(603) 863-3300

Sig Sauer
72 Pease Boulevard
Newington, NH 03801
603-610-3000
http://www.sigsauer.com/

Wilson Tactical
3989 Hwy. 62 West, Ste. 3
Berryville, AR 72616
870.423.3319
http://www.wilsontactical.com/knives.aspx

5.11 Tactical
(866) 451-1726
5.11 Inc.
4300 Spyres Way
Modesto, CA 95356
http://www.511tactical.com/

Finally, the author:
Michael W. Weissberg
305-796-6110
Miamicuffs@aol.com

Complaints, compliments, & gripes accepted. Apologies extended under certain conditions. If I left you out, and you make the world's greatest holster, and I offended you greatly, contact me. Maybe we can work together for volume 2.

Photo Gallery

These photos are to provide the reader with some basic illustration to reinforce the written material, and to allow the reader to shop at home before going to a retailer.

As a writer I bear a grave responsibility: If I were to say that I do not like a particular holster maker or his designs, I am likely to ruin his business and hurt him and his family. I have only an opinion, and it is no better or worse than yours.

As I am sure most readers will want to know what I carry personally, I have included a section on that as well. I work or have worked as a police officer, police detective, police sergeant, assistant chief, firearms instructor, private investigator, bodyguard, and troubleshooter. Each job requires or required different gear.

Knives

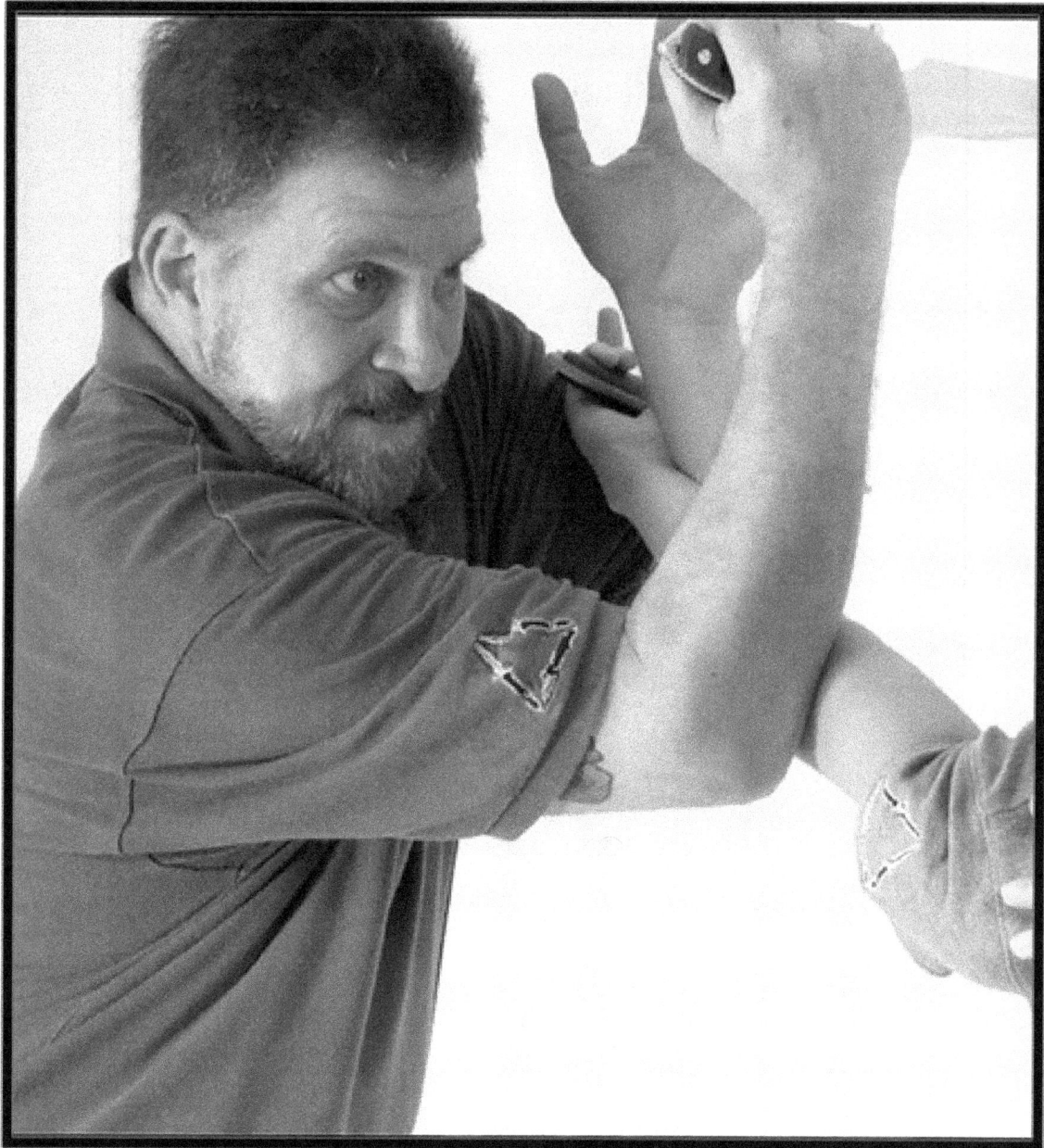

Grandmaster Bram Frank teaching a knife defense instructor seminar at the Hialeah Police Department in Hialeah, Florida

Photo credit: Michael Weissberg

The forward or "hammer" grip
Demonstrated by Grandmaster Frank
(Photo used by permission of Bram Frank)

The reverse or "ice pick" grip
Demonstrated by Grandmaster Frank
(Photo used by permission of Bram Frank)

The Filipino or "cancer grip"
Demonstrated by Grandmaster Frank
(Photo used by permission of Bram Frank)

The "fencing grip"
Demonstrated by Grandmaster Frank
(Photo used by permission of Bram Frank)

Grandmaster Bram Frank's
Siko Knife and Z'mora Knife
Manufactured by Mantis Knives
Photo credit: Michael Weissberg

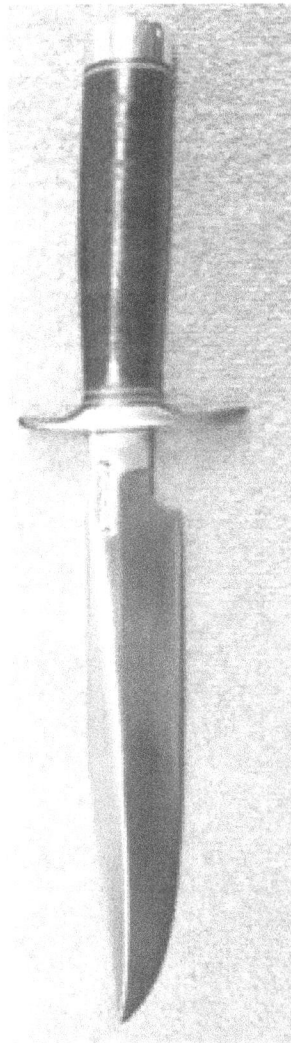

Randall Made #1 Knife
Photo credit: Michael Weissberg

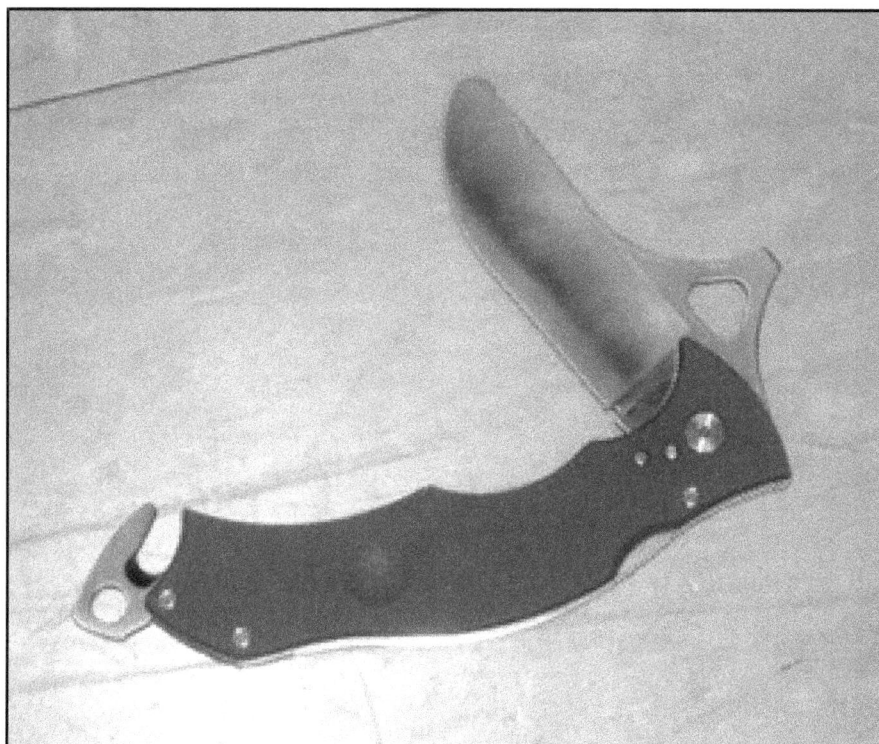

Grandmaster Bram Frank's CRIMPT, the Close Range Medium Impact Tool. The first new martial arts tool in over 100 years, designed for non-lethal police use. This tool combines the teachings of Remy Presas, Wally Jay, George Dillman, and Bram Frank.

Photo credit: Michael Weissberg

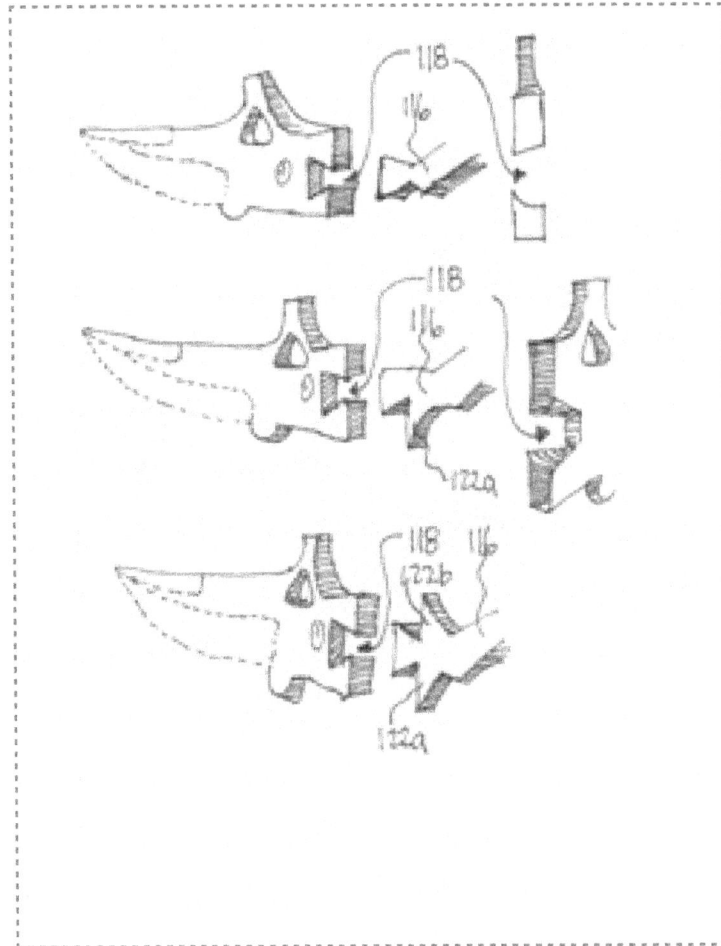

Original Sketches
Grandmaster Bram Frank's
Puzzle Lock Knife
Used by Permission from Bram Frank

Guro Michael Weissberg uses the Gunting
On Master Anthony J Pellicano.
Master Pellicano shows some level of discomfort.
Photo credit: Bram Frank

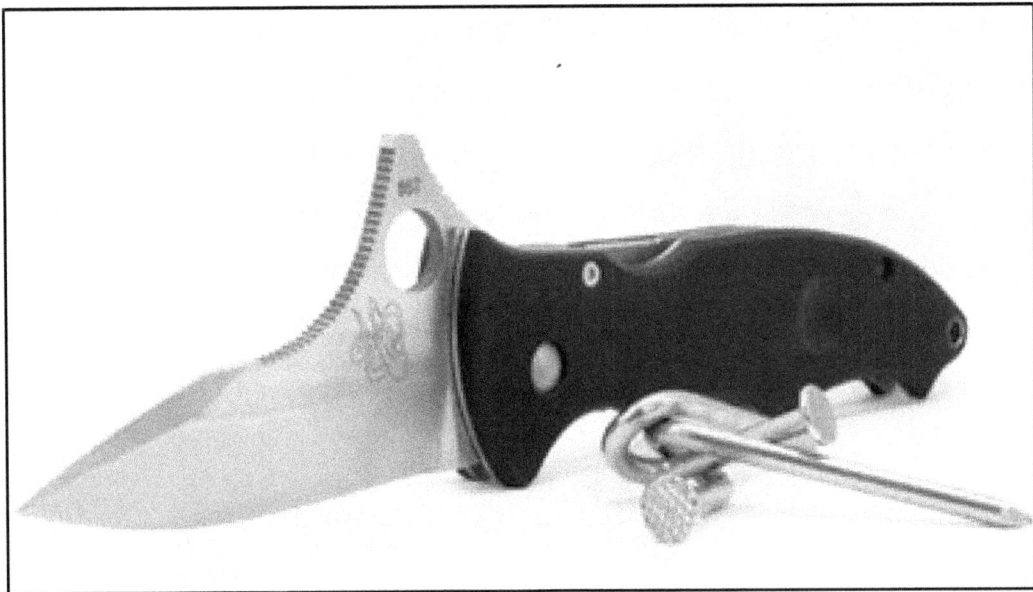

Grandmaster Bram Frank's
Gunting Knife
Photo credit: Bram Frank

Grandmaster Bram Frank's
Lapu-Lapu Corto Knife
Photo credit: Bram Frank

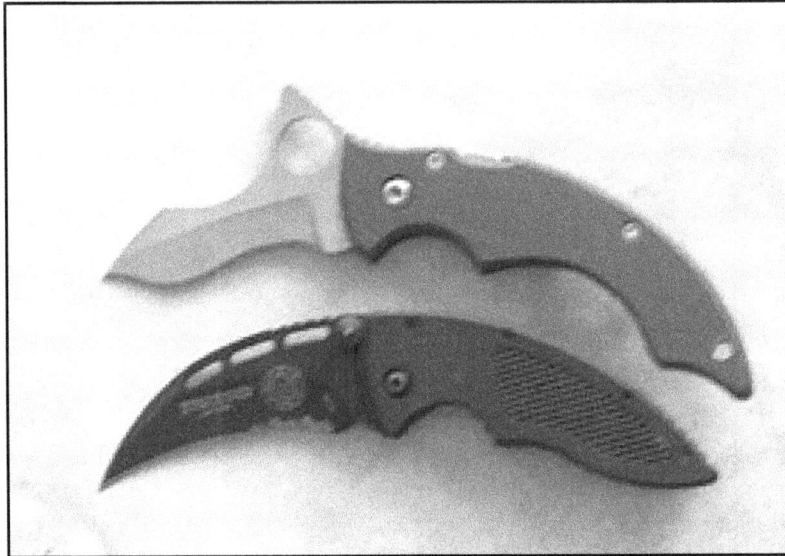

Grandmaster Bram Frank's Tusok Knife (Top)
Grandmaster Graciela Casillas'
Ladyhawk Knife (Bottom)
Photo credit: Bram Frank

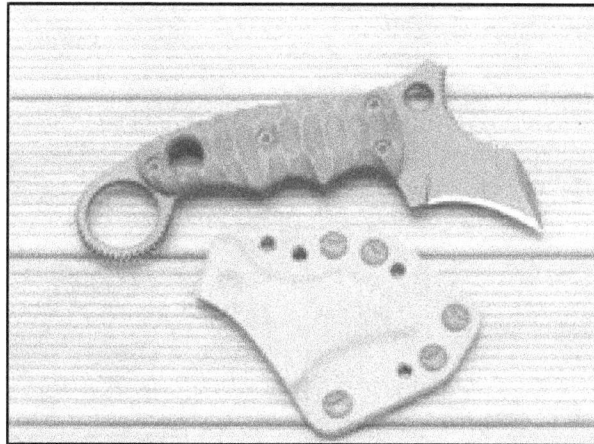

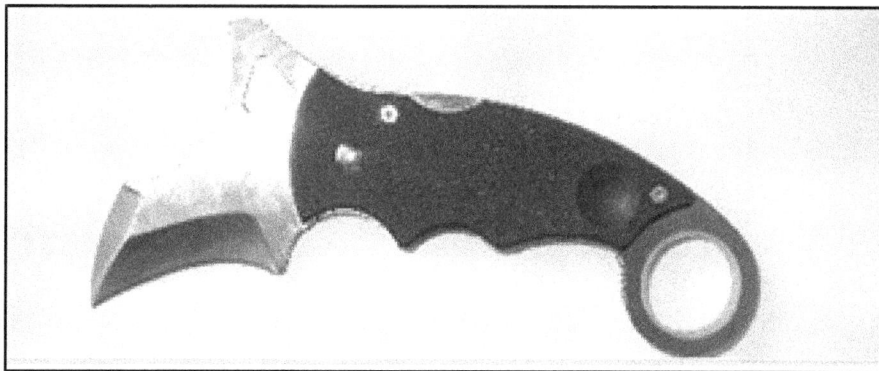

Grandmaster Bram Frank's Desangut Knife
Fixed Blade (top) Folding Blade (Bottom)
Photo credit: Bram Frank

Grandmaster Bram Frank's Abaniko Knife
Photo credit: Bram Frank

Bowen Belt Buckle Knife
Photo credit: Bowen Knives.

M16-14SFG Tanto Designed by Kit Carson (top)
M21-14DSFG Designed by Kit Carson (Bottom)
Photo credit: Michael Weissberg

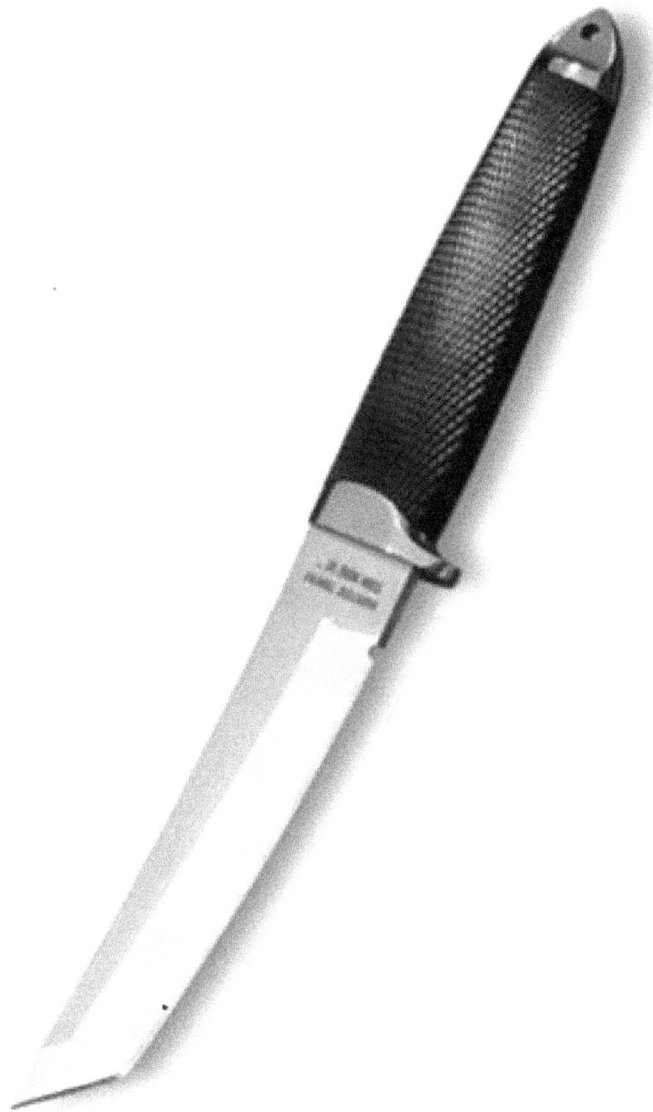

Cold Steel's Tanto Knife
Photo credit: Michael Weissberg

Gerber MK 1 Knife
Photo credit: Michael Weissberg

Al Mar "Wild Hair" Dagger Knife
Photo credit: Michael Weissberg

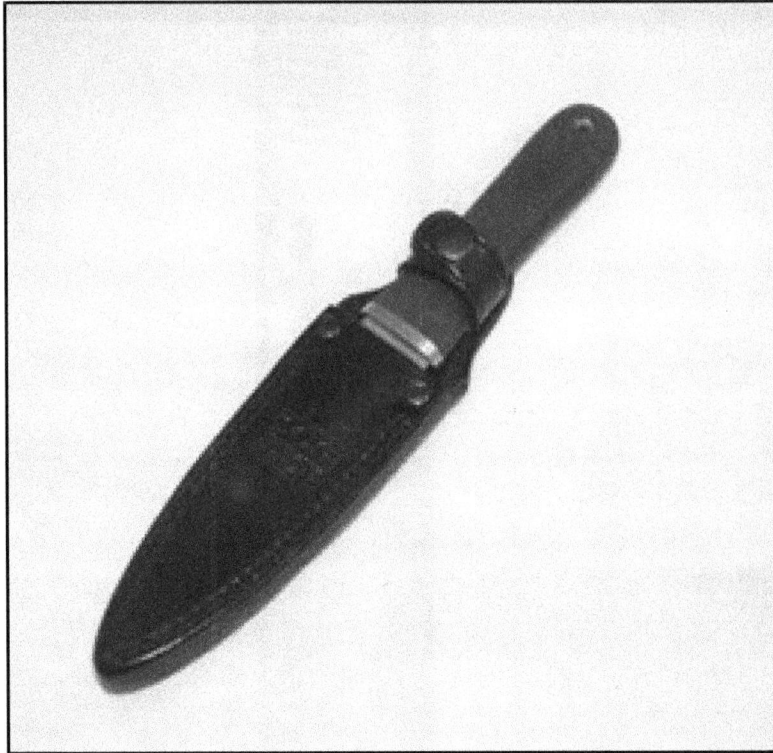

SOG Pentagon Boot Knife
(old style leather scabbard)
Photo credit: Michael Weissberg

Spyderco Police Model
(Photo Credit: Michael Weissberg)

Holsters

How A Holster is Made

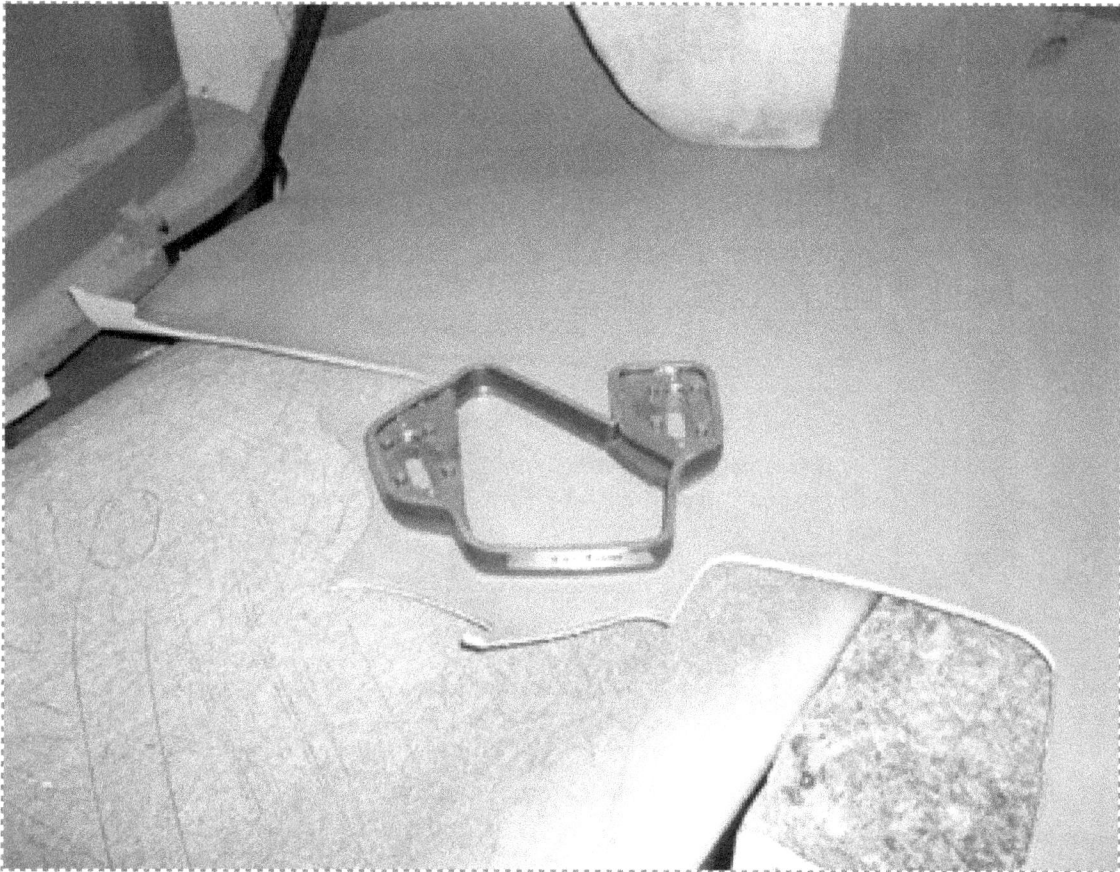

Belly leather is die cut or hand cut

How A Holster is Made

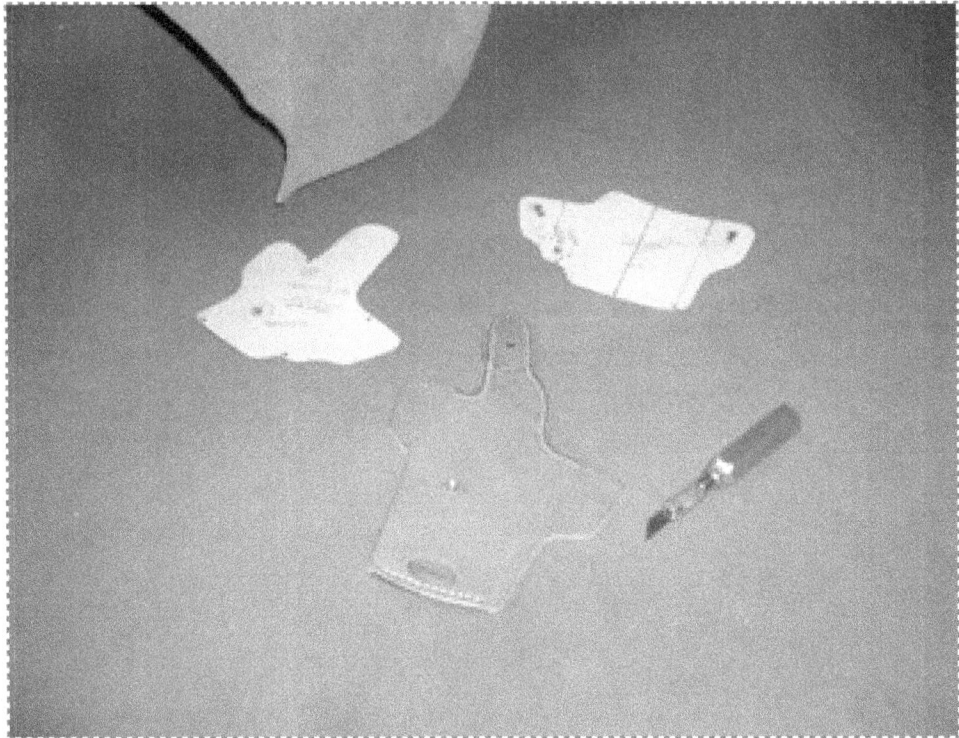

Belly leather is hand cut using a paper pattern

How A Holster is Made

A patterned holster

How A Holster is Made

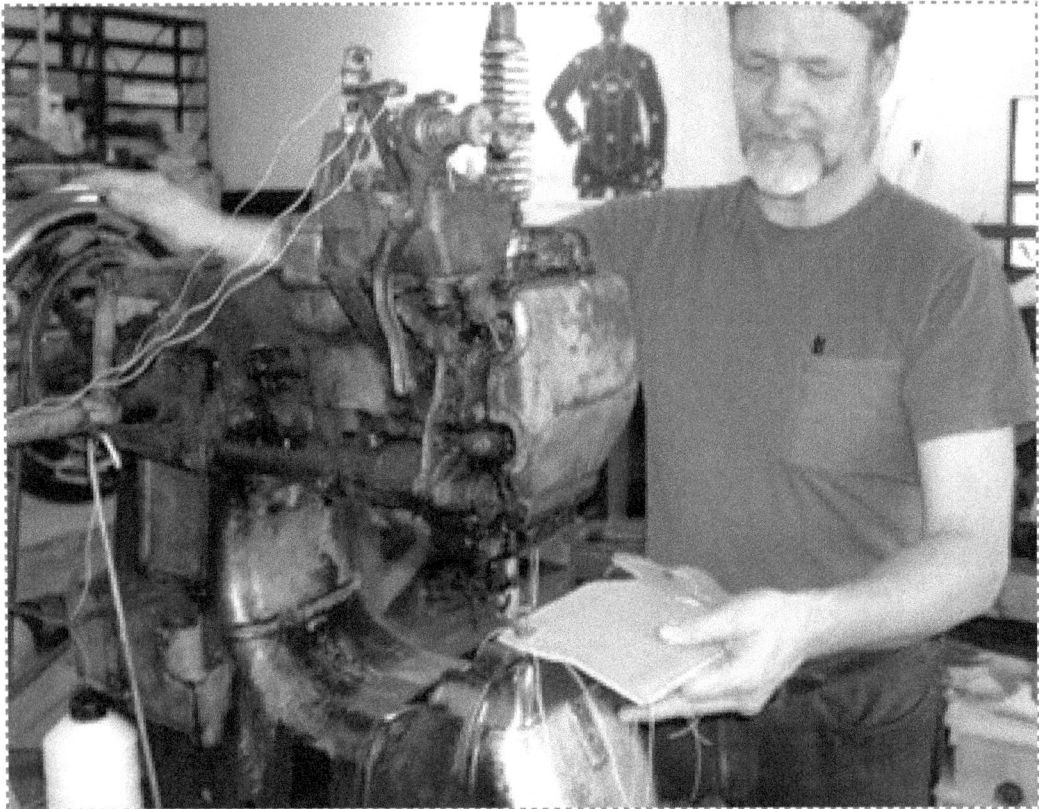

Hand stitching a holster together

How A Holster is Made

Hand stitching a holster together

How A Holster is Made

Hand setting the hardware

How A Holster is Made

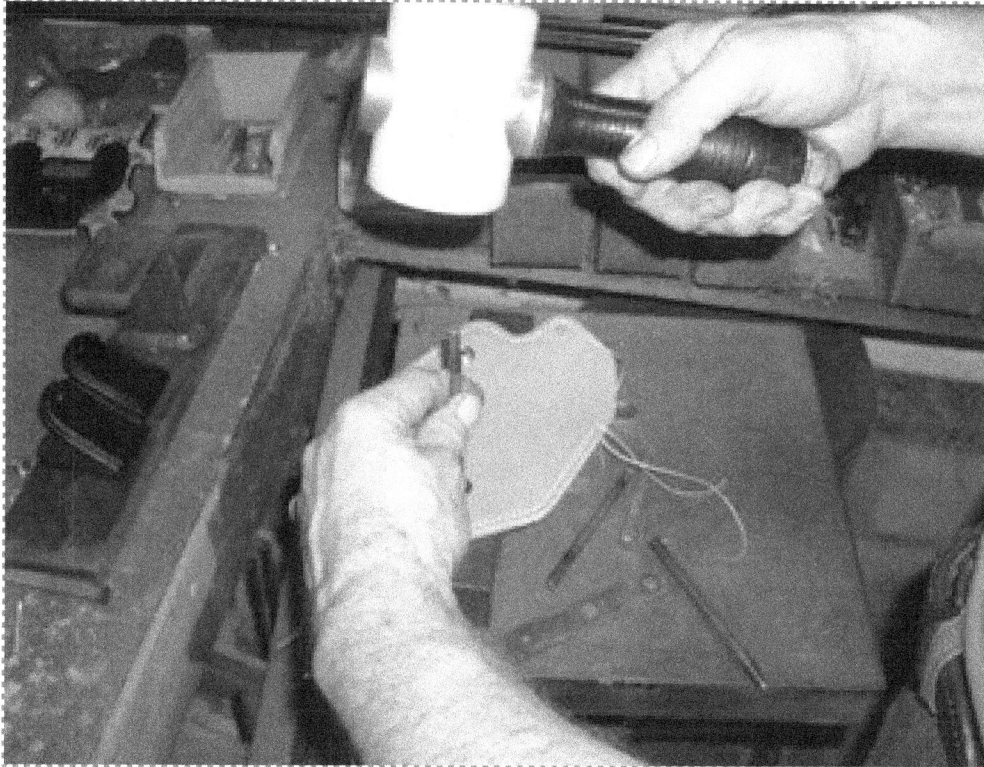

Hand setting the hardware

How A Holster is Made

Using a pot metal molded gun to wet mold the leather

How A Holster is Made

pot metal molded Taurus Judge

How A Holster is Made

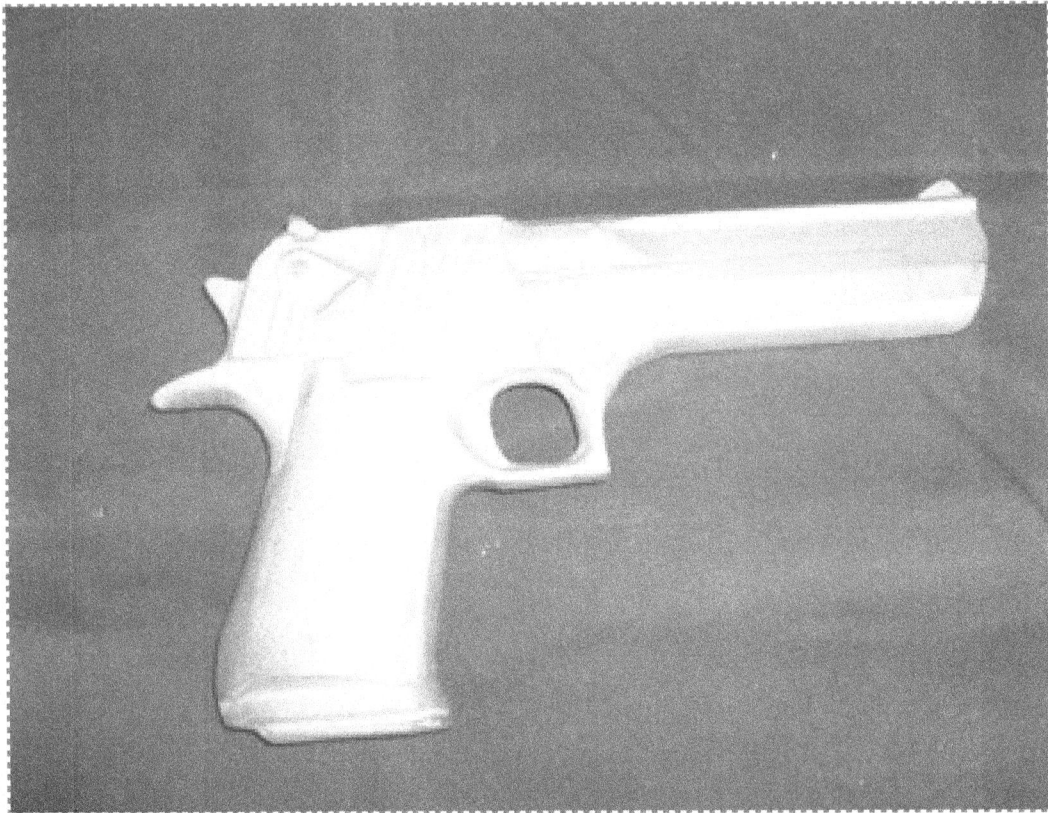

pot metal molded Desert Eagle

How A Holster is Made

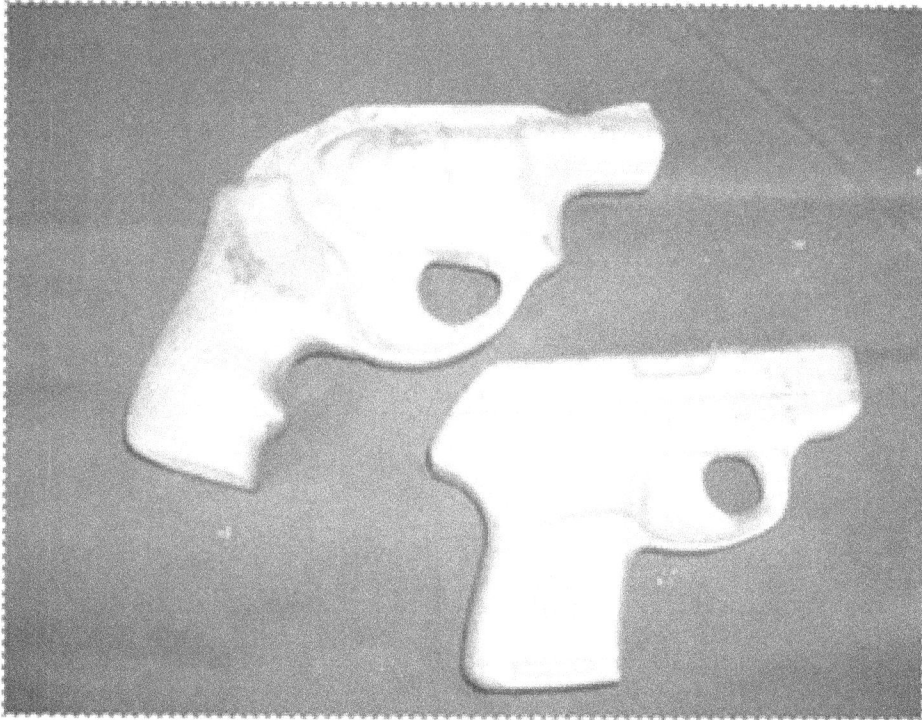

Pot metal molded Ruger and Kel Tec

How A Holster is Made

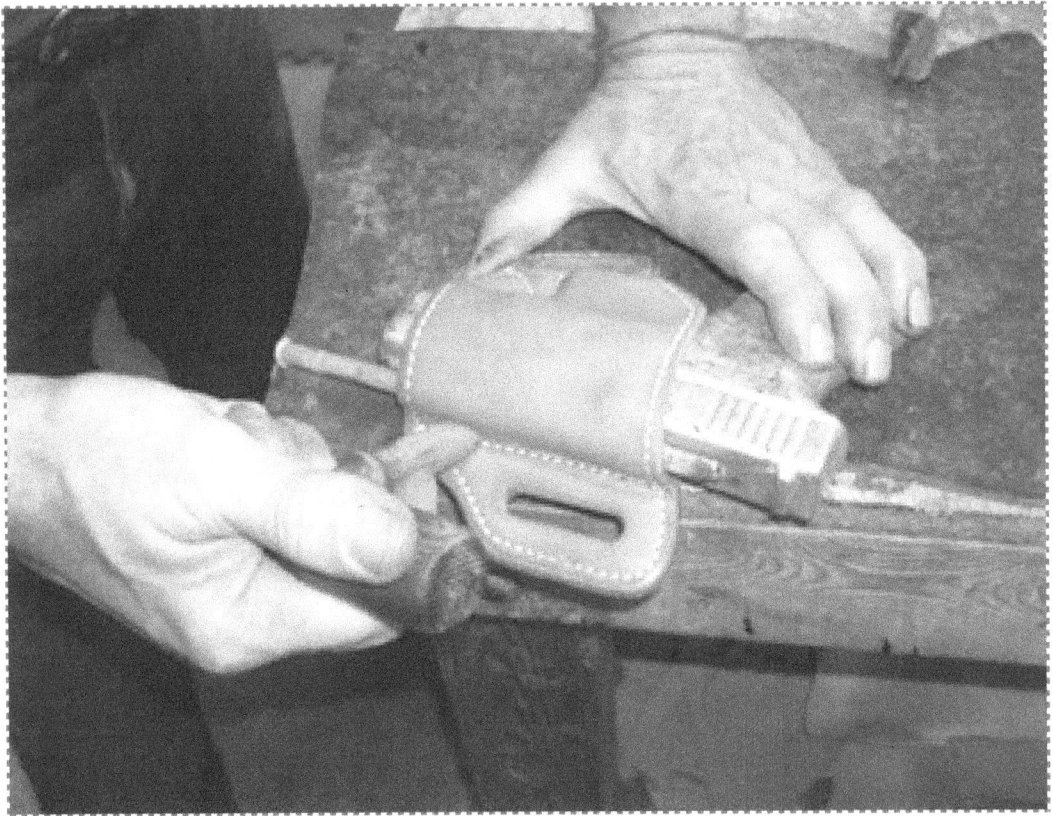

Hand Boning to get the shape of the gun.
The rod adds a sight channel

How A Holster is Made

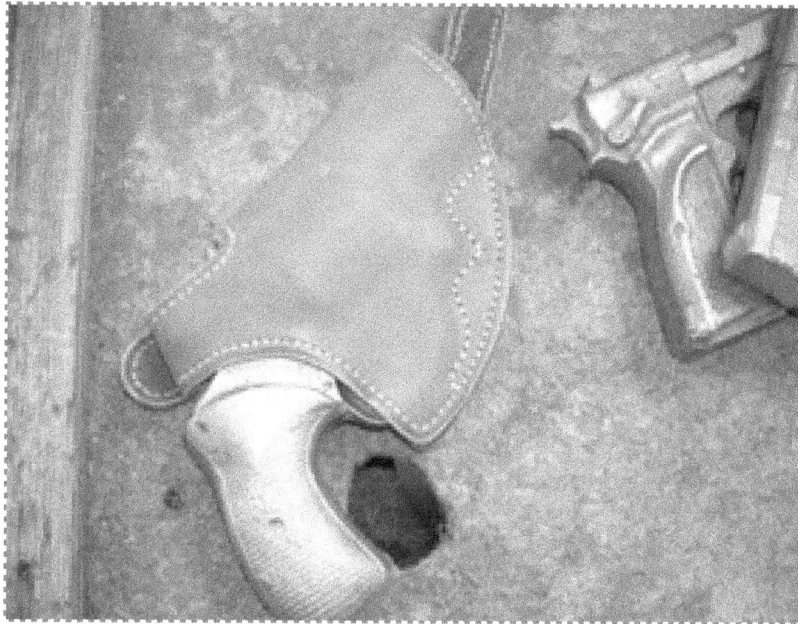

Hand Boning to get the shape of the gun

How A Holster is Made

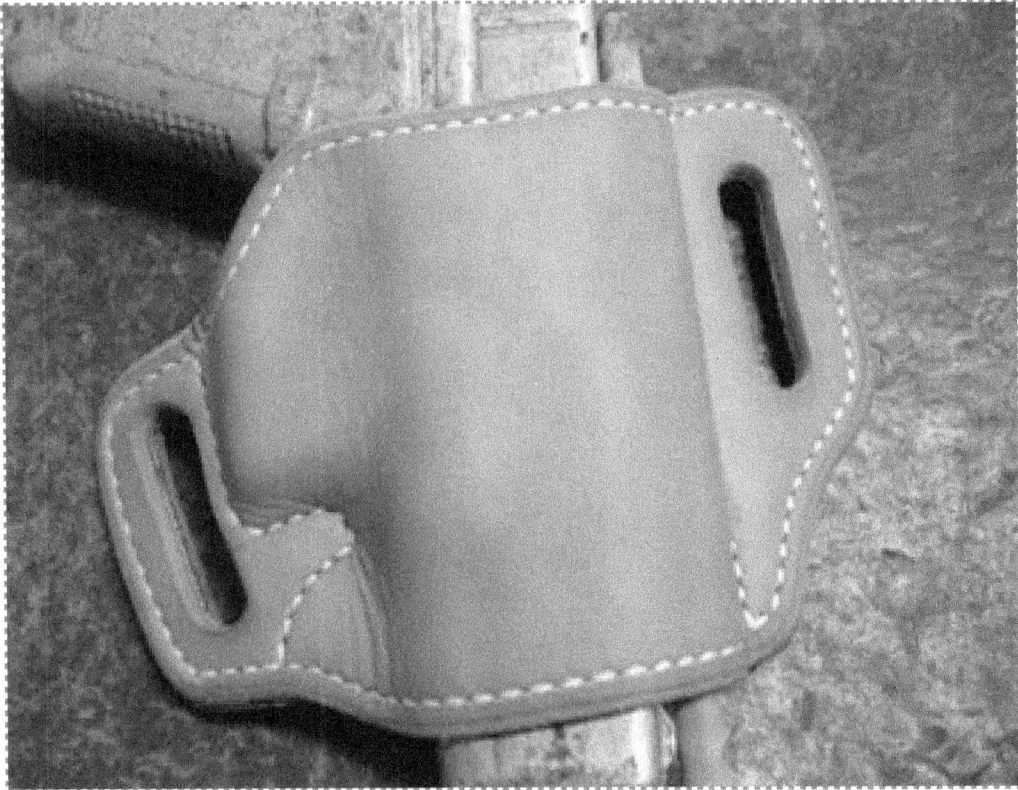

Before boning

How A Holster is Made

Ready for dye

How A Holster is Made

Applying dye by hand
This is a magazine pouch

How A Holster is Made

Hand setting hardware

How A Holster is Made

Adjusting a tensioning screw

How A Holster is Made

The finished product,
And the artisan who made it
Master Holster maker Sam Andrews

How A Holster is Made

Holsters waiting to ship out

How A Holster is Made

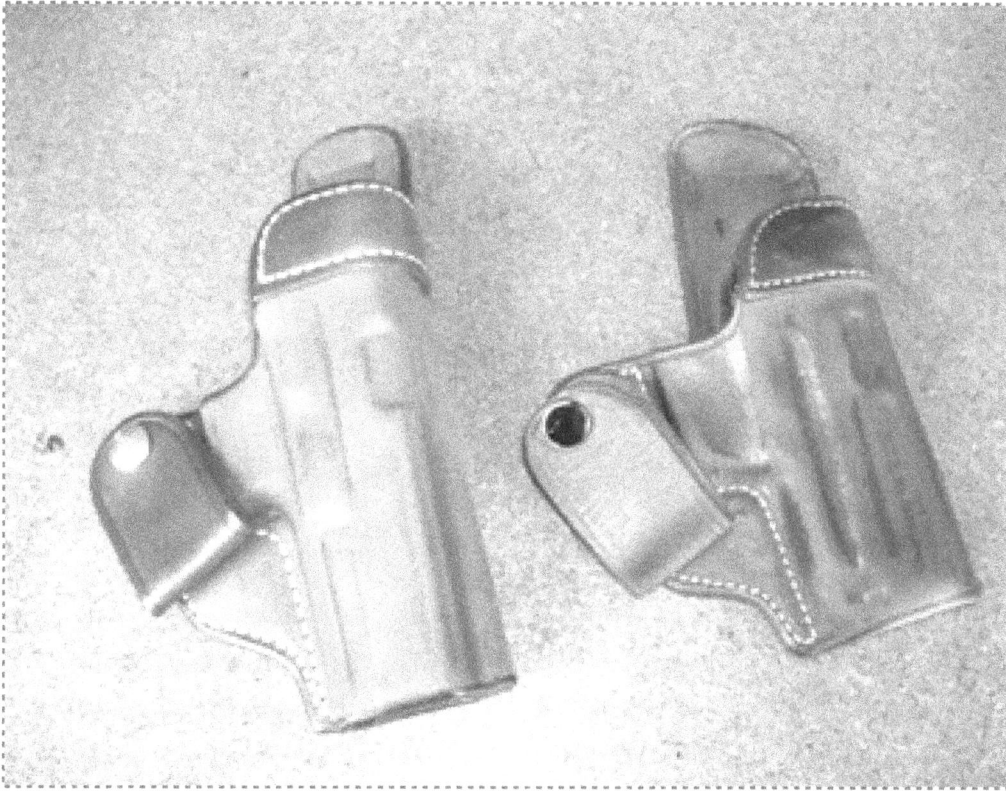

The proof:
A new McDaniel (Left)
A McDaniel carried by Firearms Instructor
Alan Koral for 20 years (right)

How a Kydex Holster is Made

Using a Rings Blue Gun as a form
(Photo Credit: Michael Weissberg)

How a Kydex Holster is Made

Using a Blackhawk Demonstrator Gun as a form
(Photo Credit: Michael Weissberg)

How a Kydex Holster is Made

Using an ASP Red Gun as a form,
A dowel is taped on to make a sight channel

(Photo Credit: Michael Weissberg)

How a Kydex Holster is Made

The ASP Red Gun is taped,
To allow it to be separated from the Kydex later
(Photo Credit: Michael Weissberg)

How a Kydex Holster is Made

The Kydex sheet is scored and cut by hand
(Photo Credit: Michael Weissberg)

How a Kydex Holster is Made

Kydex sheets are heated in an oven
(Photo Credit: Michael Weissberg)

How a Kydex Holster is Made

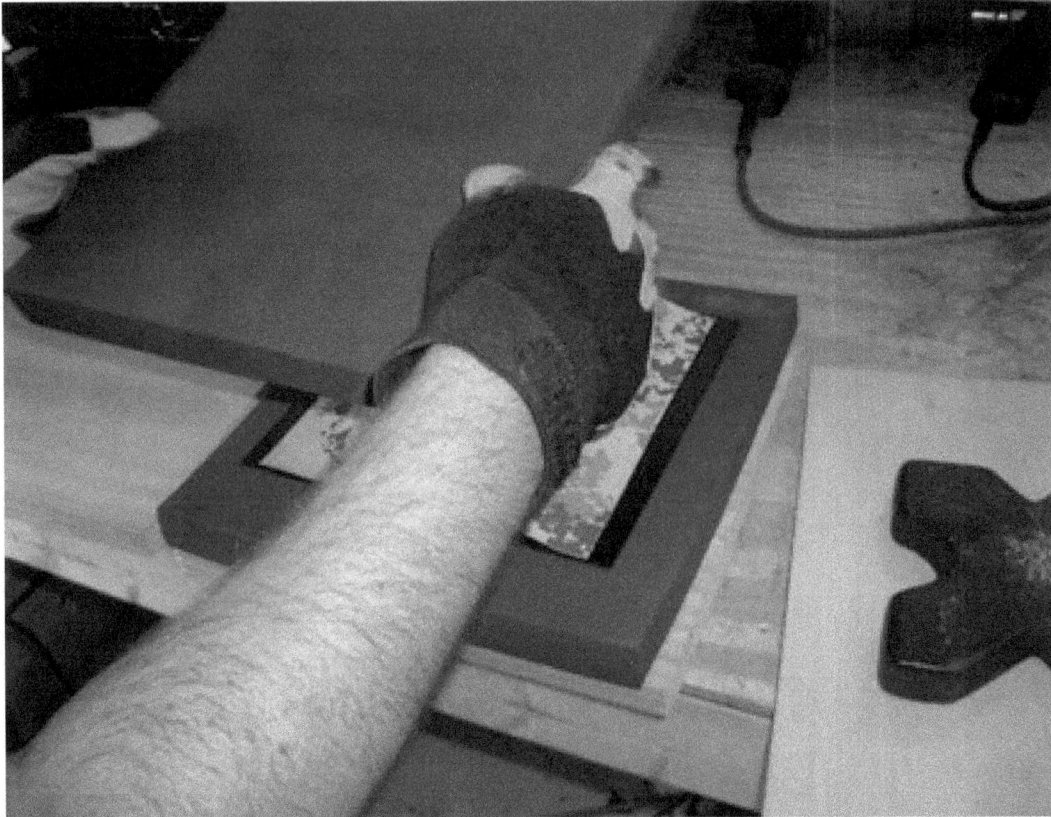

The second Kydex sheet is placed on top
and sandwiched between dense foam plates

(Photo Credit: Michael Weissberg)

How a Kydex Holster is Made

Wood is placed on top and bottom
sandwiching the dense foam plates
(Photo Credit: Michael Weissberg)

How a Kydex Holster is Made

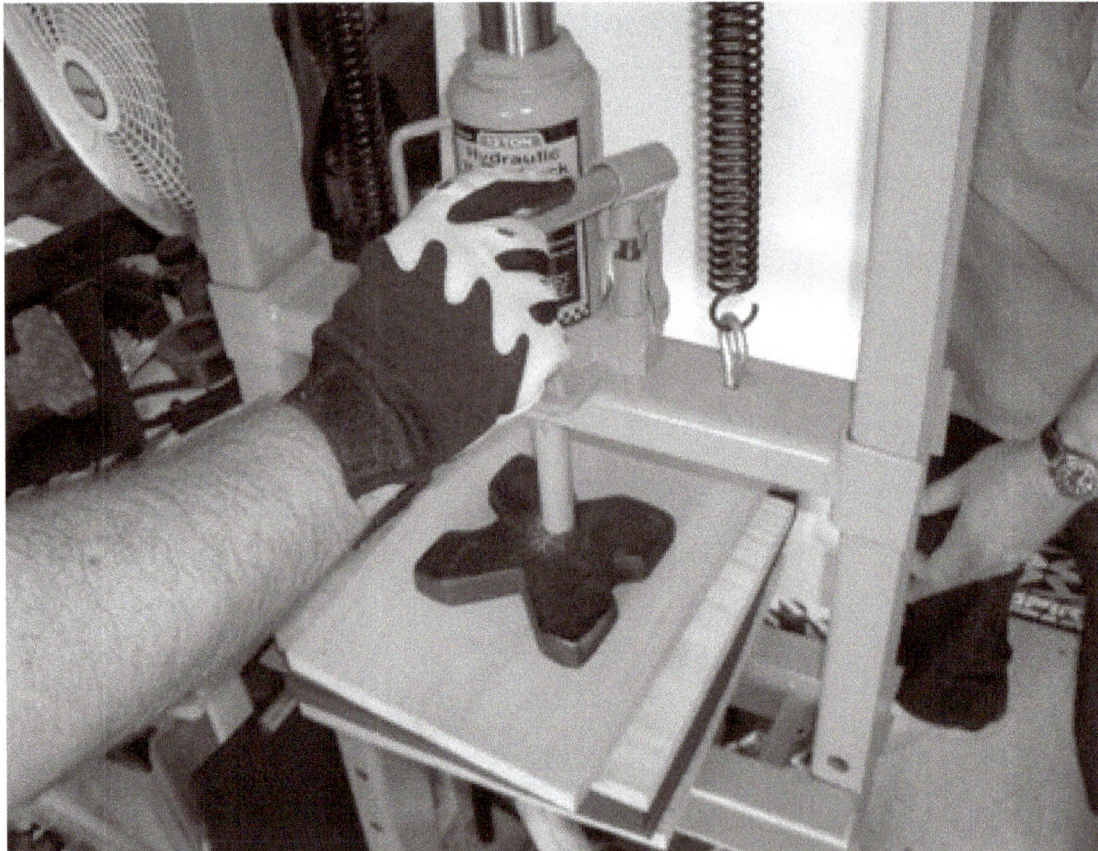

A hydraulic press makes the Kydex mold to the form
(Photo Credit: Michael Weissberg)

How a Kydex Holster is Made

The holster is trimmed

(Photo Credit: Michael Weissberg)

How a Kydex Holster is Made

The holster is riveted together
(Photo Credit: Michael Weissberg)

How a Kydex Holster is Made

The hardware is added

(Photo Credit: Michael Weissberg)

How a Kydex Holster is Made

Randy Levine of Crossfire Holsters
shows the finished holster

(Photo Credit: Michael Weissberg)

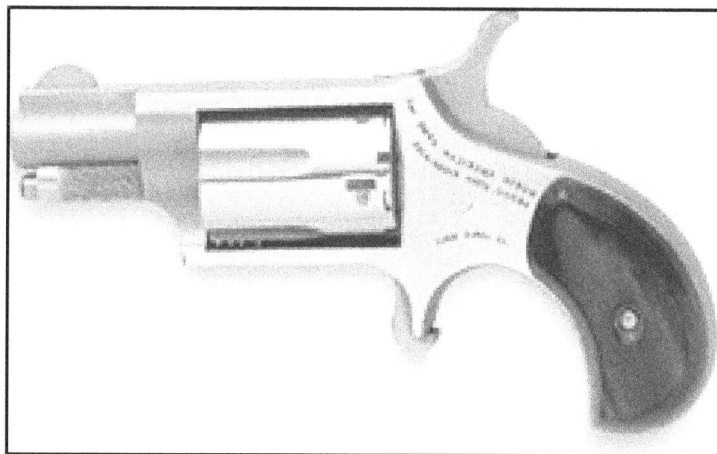

NAA Derringer with belt buckle
NAA Derringer
Photo credit: Michael Weissberg

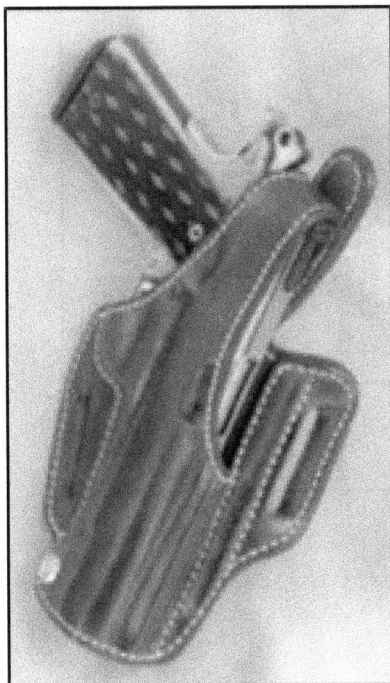

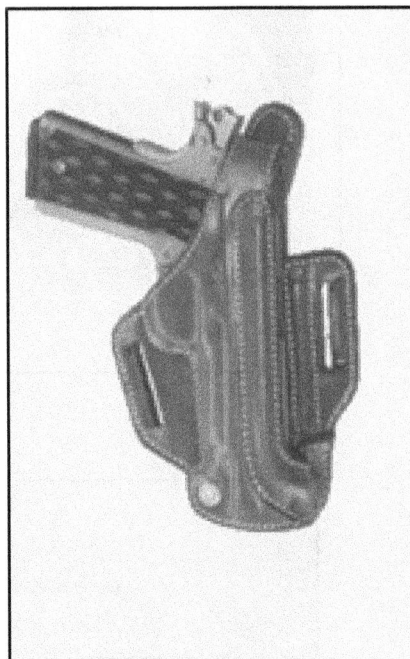

Sam Andrews Hybrid Saddle Holster
Sam Andrews IPSC Pancake Holster
Photo credit: Sam Andrews

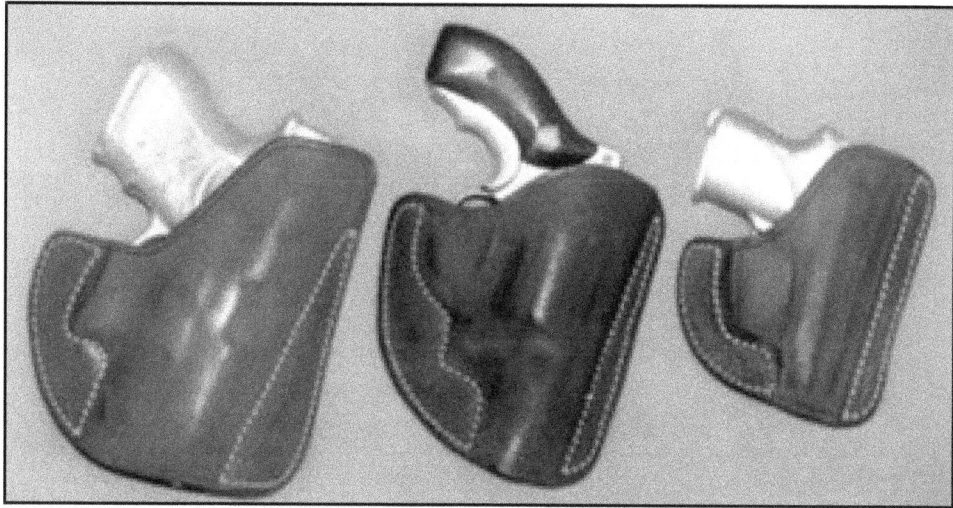

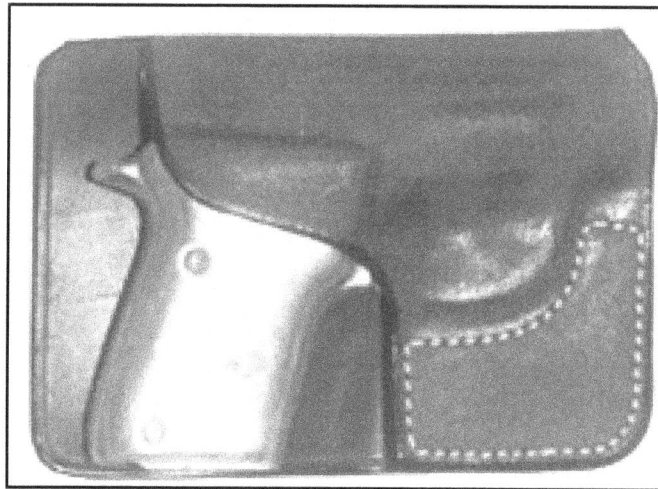

Sam Andrews Front Pocket Holsters
Sam Andrews Back Pocket Holster
Photo credit: Sam Andrews

Sam Andrews Pocket Holsters
Beretta .32 and Beretta .25
These "mouse guns" are meant as 2nd or 3rd guns
Photo credit: Michael Weissberg

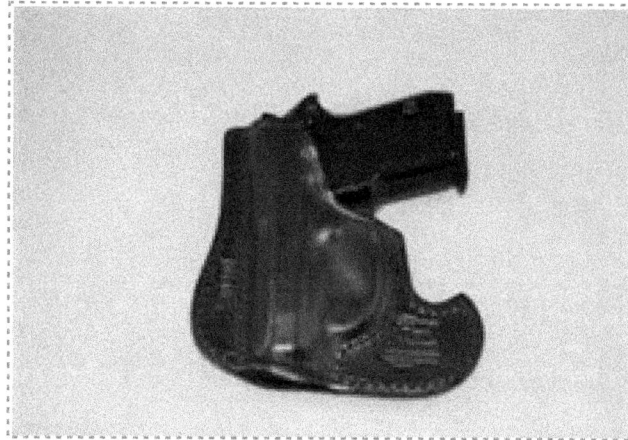

Don Hume Pocket Holsters
Beretta .32 and Beretta .25
These "mouse guns" are meant as 2nd or 3rd guns
Photo credit: Michael Weissberg

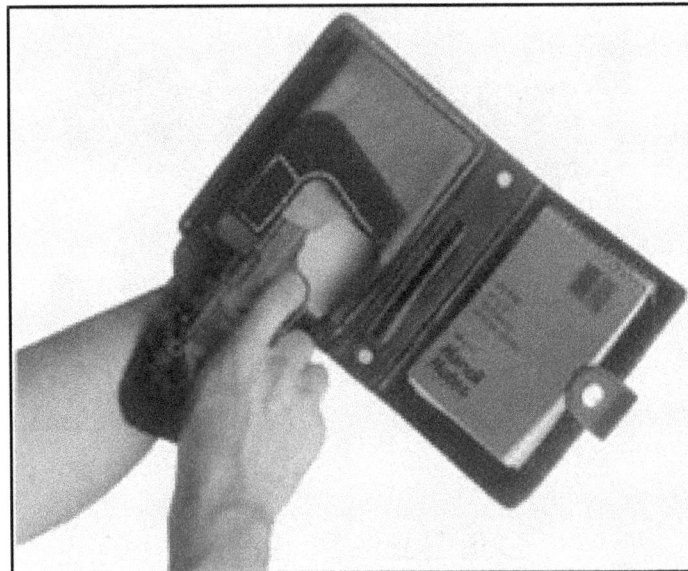

Sam Andrews Notebook Holster
Photo credit: Sam Andrews

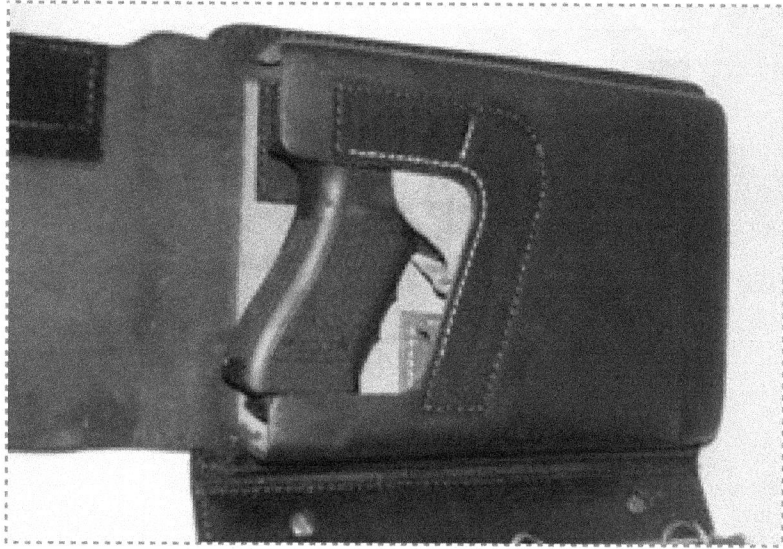

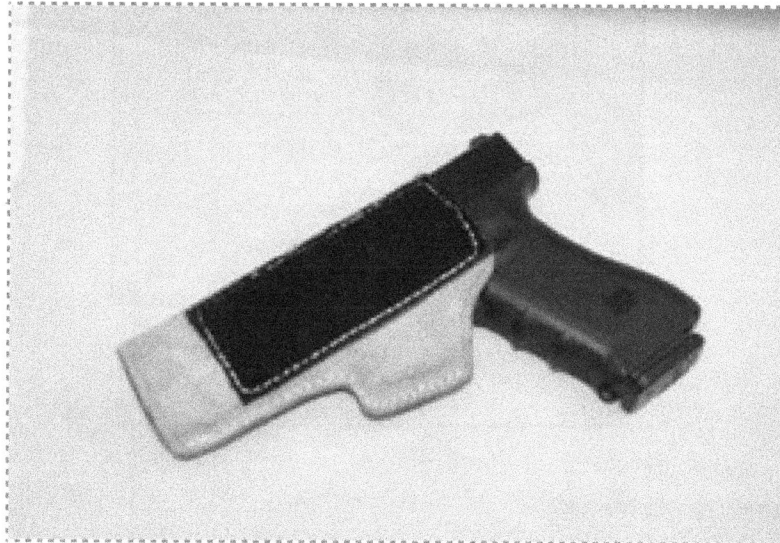

Glock 22 in Andrews' Notebook
Top photo shows liner holster
Photo credit: Michael Weissberg

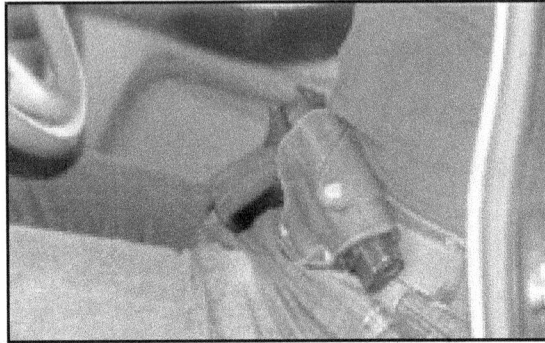

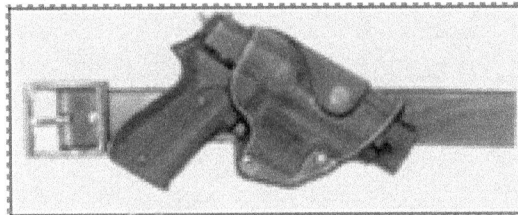

Sam Andrews Carjacker Holster
Photo credit: Sam Andrews

162

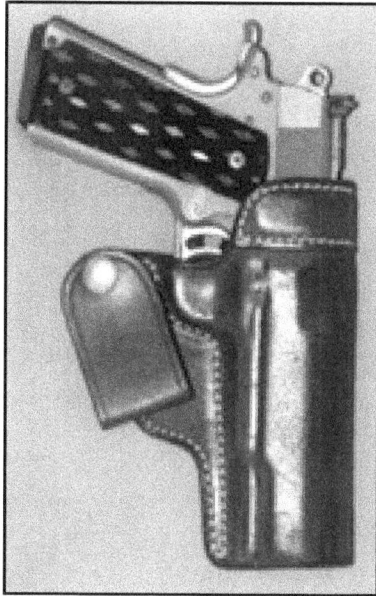

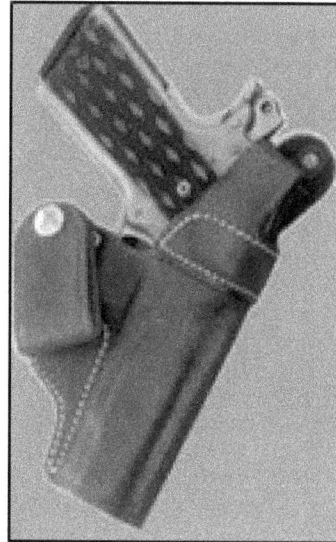

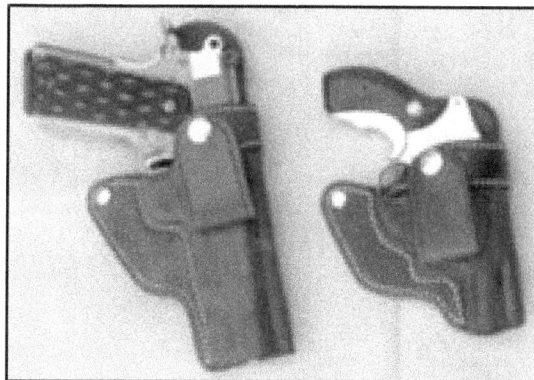

Sam Andrews Inside-the-pants Holsters
(McDaniel Style)
Photo credit: Sam Andrews

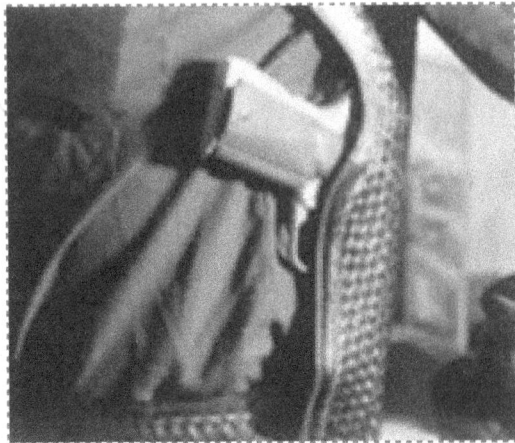

Sam Andrews Spring-break Vertical Shoulder Holster
Photo credit: Sam Andrews

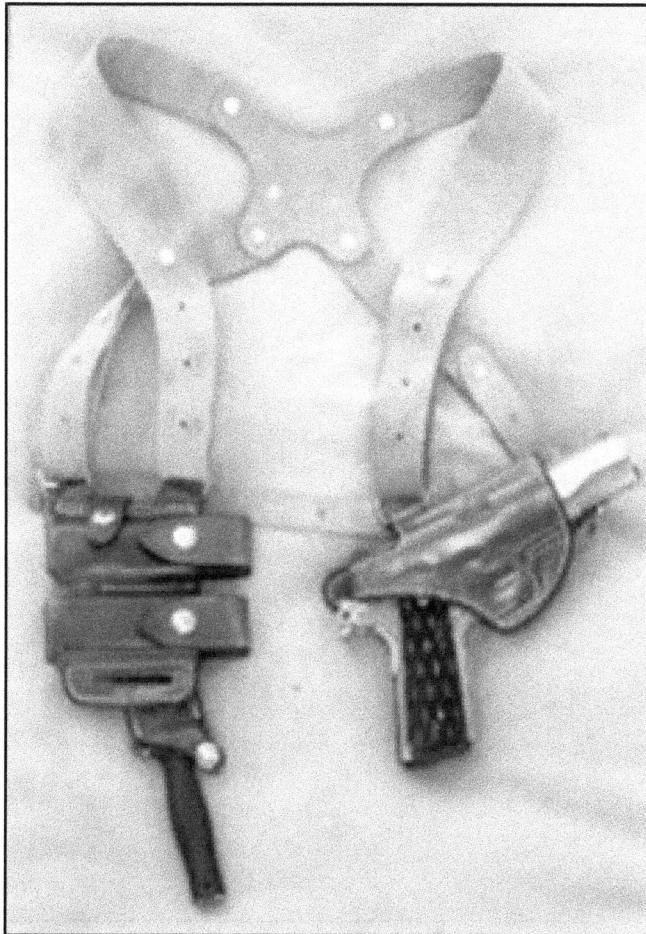

Sam Andrews Monarch Shoulder Holster
Note: Extra Magazine Holder, Knife Holder
Photo credit: Sam Andrews

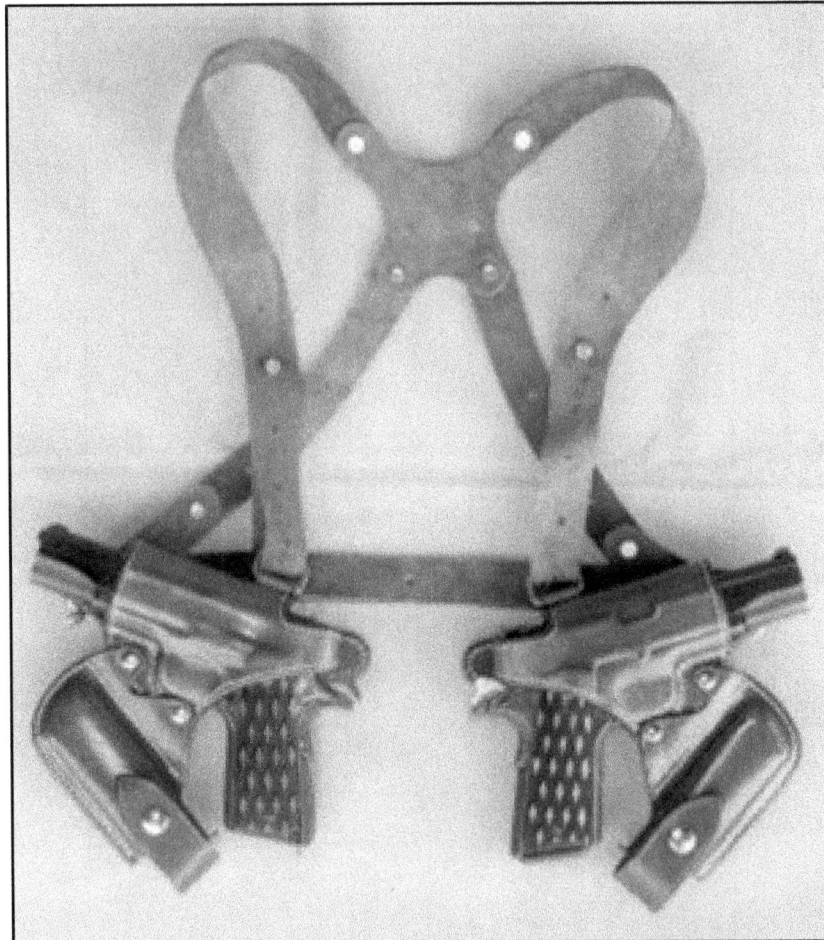

Sam Andrews Urban Safari Shoulder Holster
Note: Extra Magazine Holder,
Backup Gun Holster
Photo credit: Sam Andrews

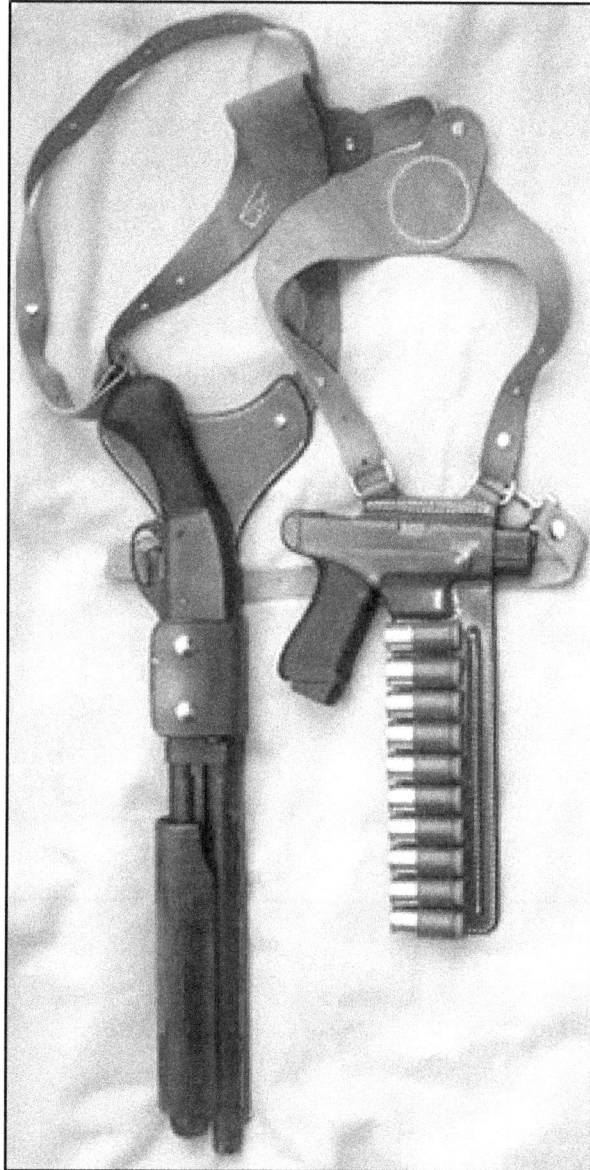

Sam Andrews Firepower Class 3 Shoulder Holster
NFA Rules Apply to Shotgun
Law Enforcement Only
Photo credit: Sam Andrews

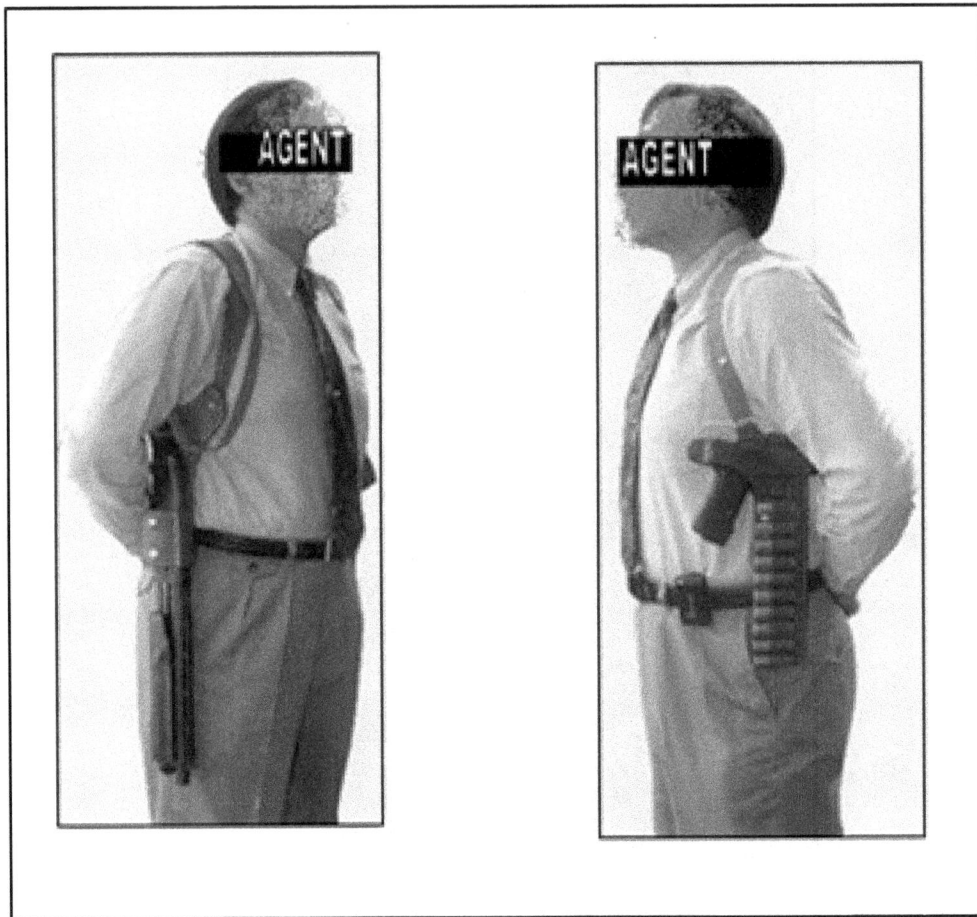

Sam Andrews Firepower Class 3 Shoulder Holster
NFA Rules Apply to Shotgun
Law Enforcement Only
Photo credit: Sam Andrews

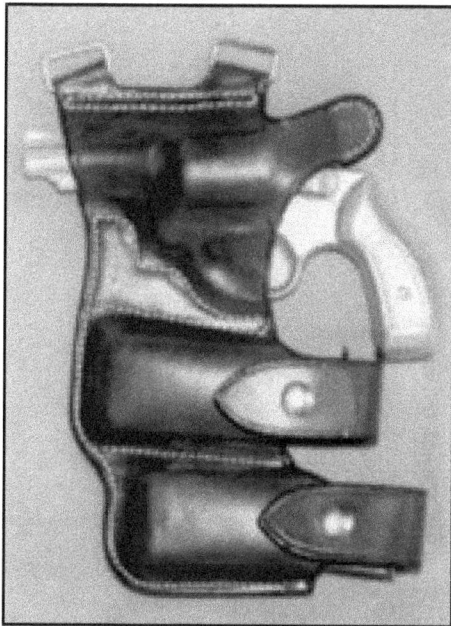

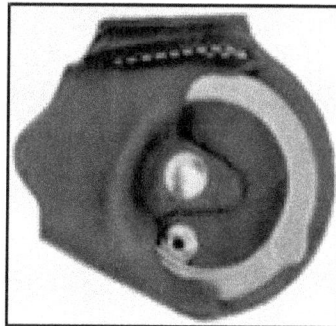

Sam Andrews Off-side Options For
Shoulder Holsters
Photo credit: Sam Andrews

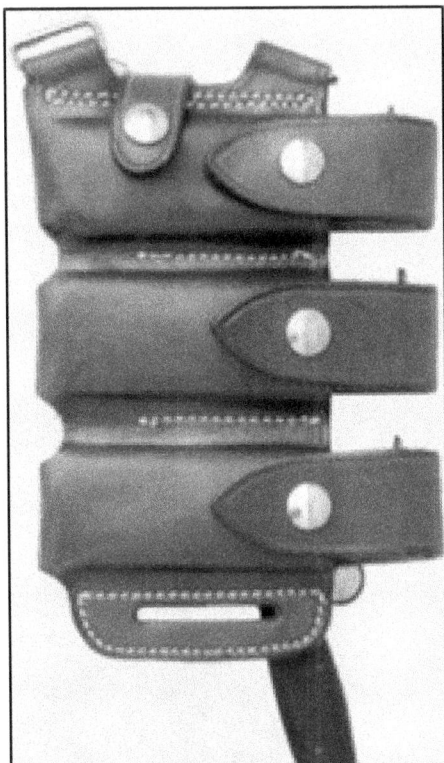

Sam Andrews Off-side Options For
Shoulder Holsters
Photo credit: Sam Andrews

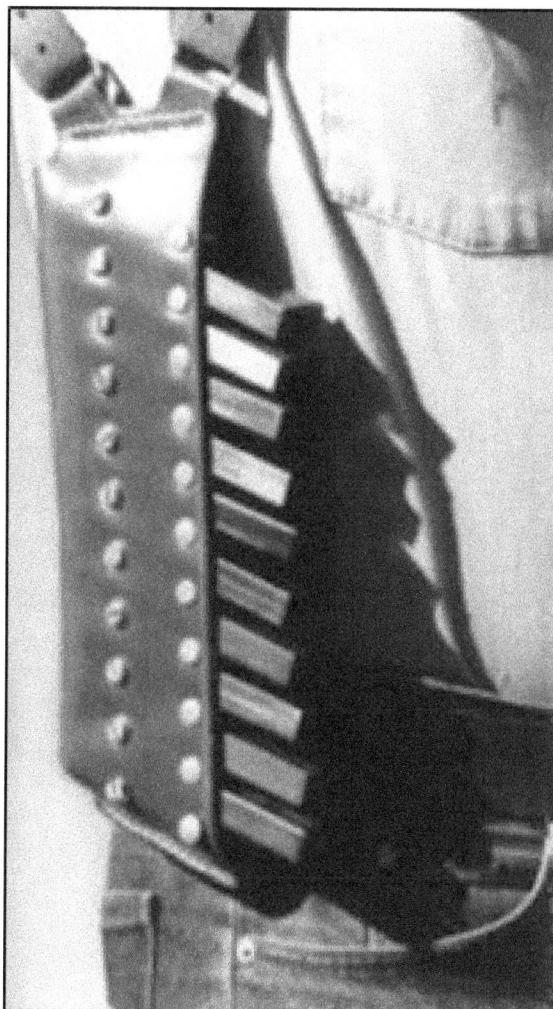

Sam Andrews Off-side Options For
Shoulder Holsters: The Stroud Ten Pack
Photo credit: Sam Andrews

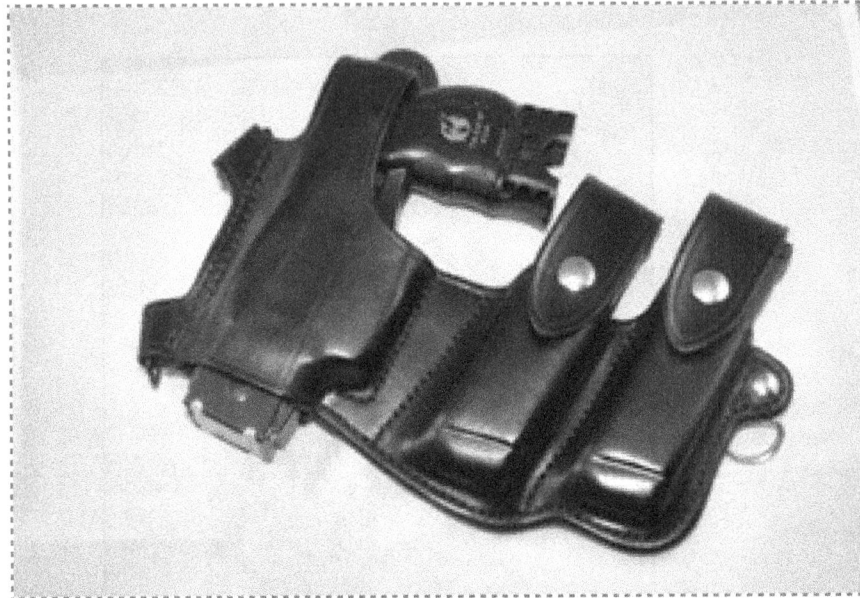

The Weissberg "Shock and Awe"
Shoulder Holster Offside (Prototype)
X26 TASER and 2 Glock 22 magazines
(This is the first time this has been seen in print)
Photo credit: Michael Weissberg

Galco's SOB (Small of the Back) Holster
Photo credit: Michael Weissberg

Galco's Ankle Glove Holster
Photo credit: Michael Weissberg

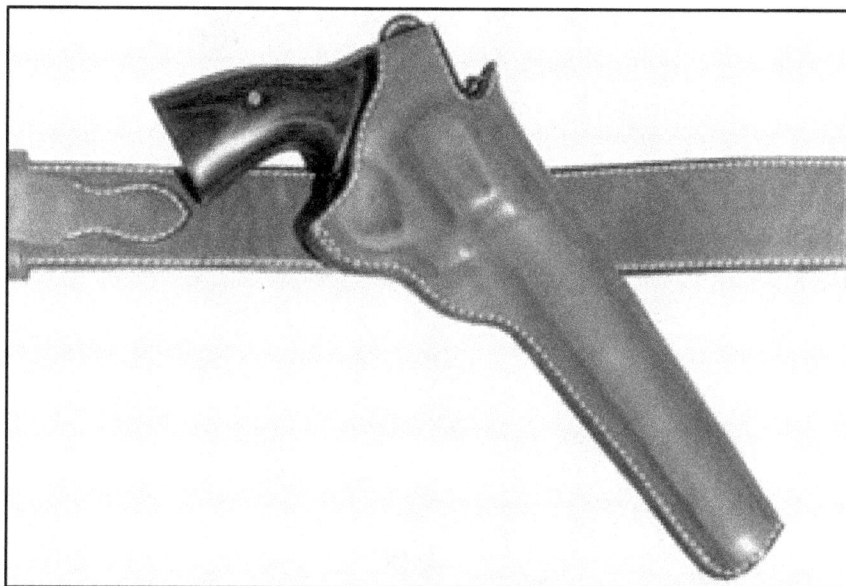

Sam Andrews Cross draw Holster
Photo credit: Sam Andrews

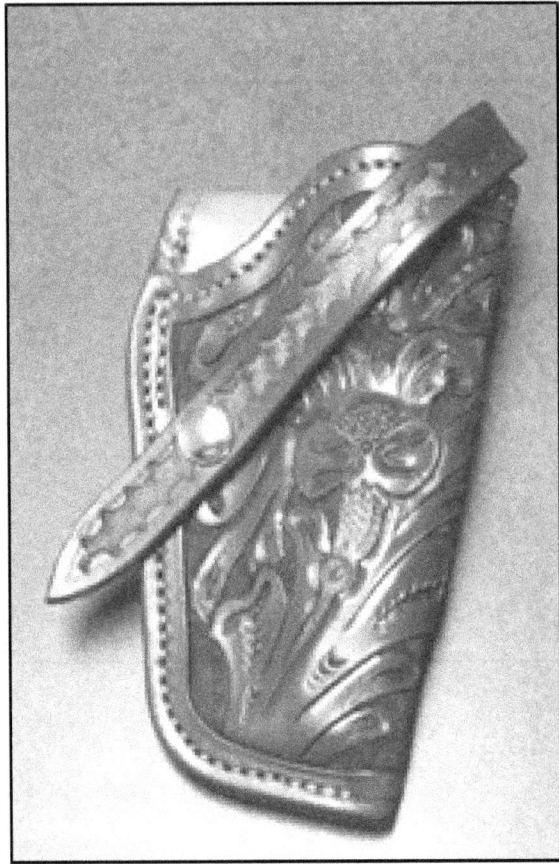

Classic Tom Threepersons Holster
Made by Lobo Gun Leather

BlackHawk Compact Slide with Mag Pouch
Photo credit: Michael Weissberg

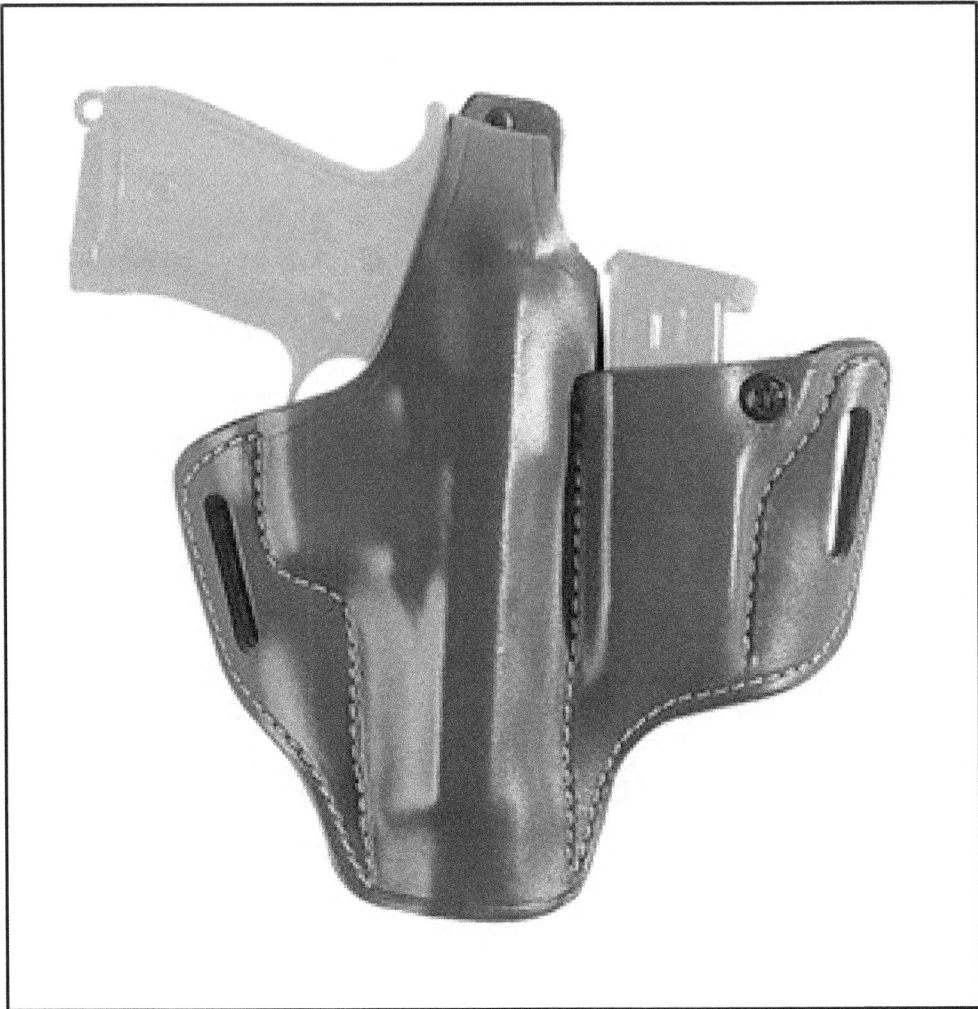

Gould and Goodrich Pancake Holster
with Mag Pouch (Galls Exclusive)

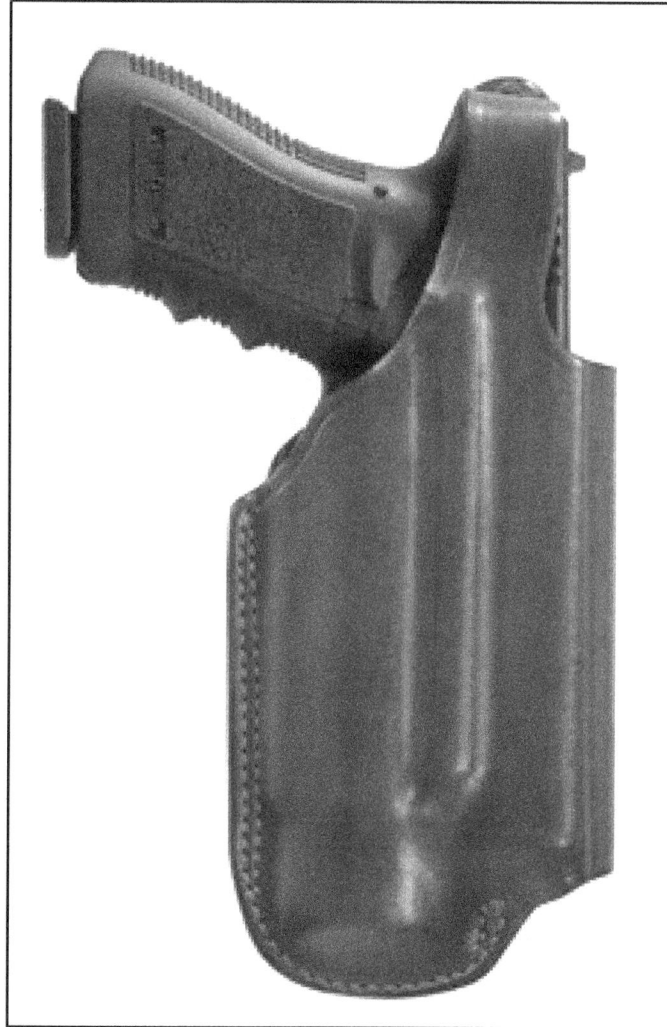

Bianchi
Vision Leather Holster For
Light Mounted Weapons
Photo Credit: Bianchi Press Releases

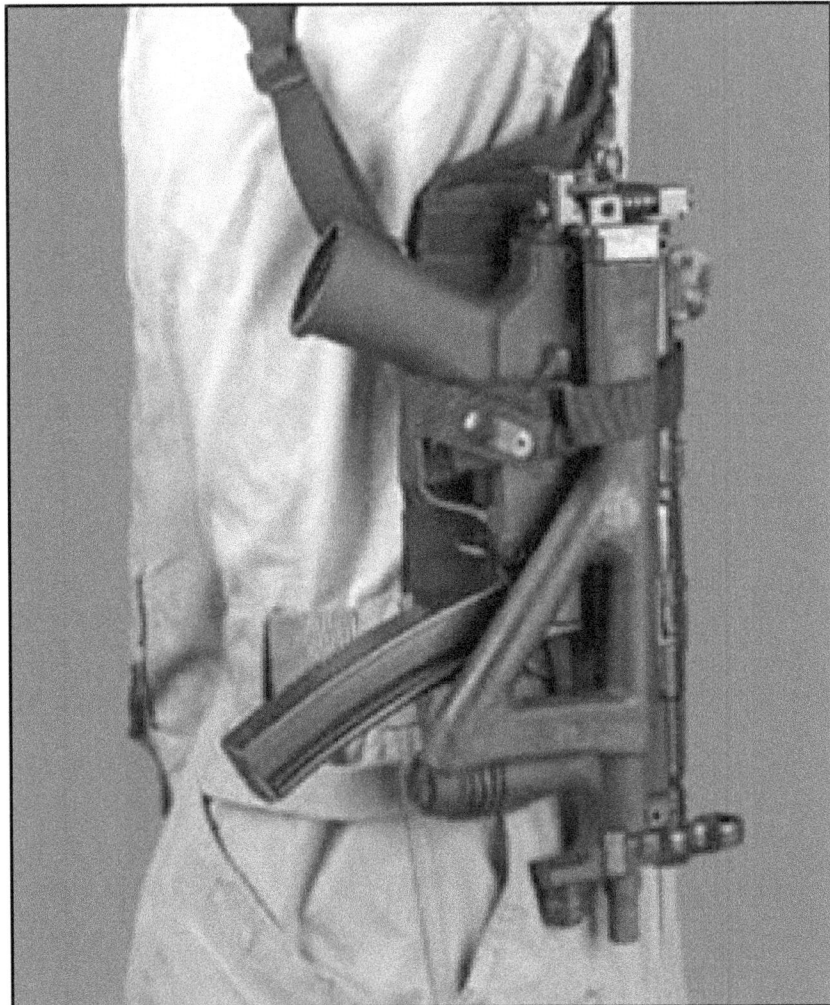

DeSantis Diplomatic Security Detail (DSD)
Submachine Gun Shoulder Rig
Photo credit: DeSantis

DeSantis Diplomatic Security Detail (DSD)
Submachine Gun Shoulder Rig
Photo credit: DeSantis

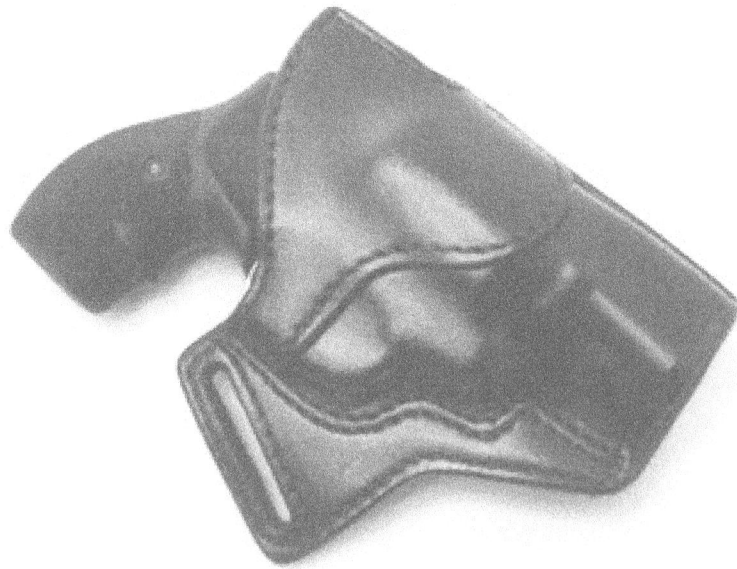

J Frame Holsters
by Don Hume

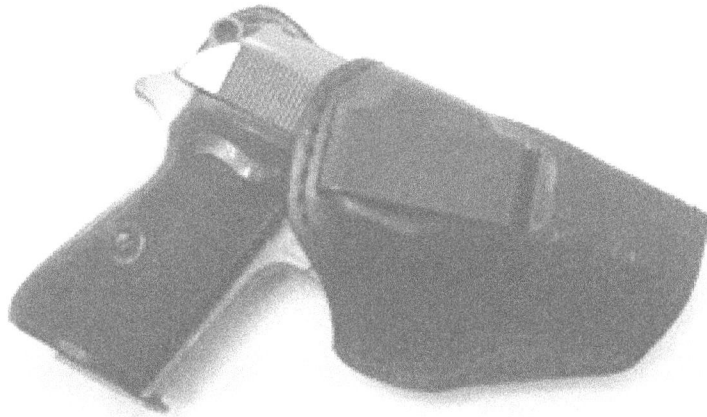

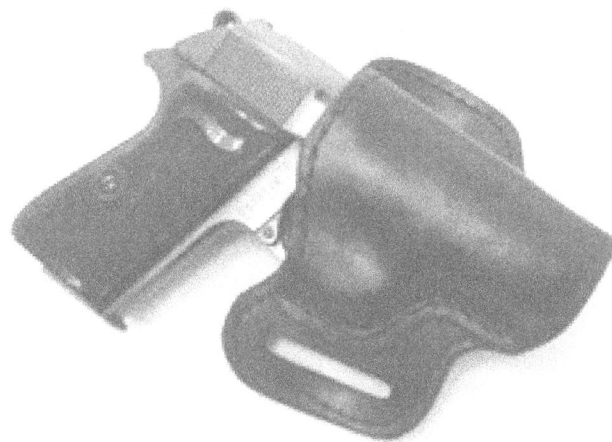

PPKS Holsters by Mernicke

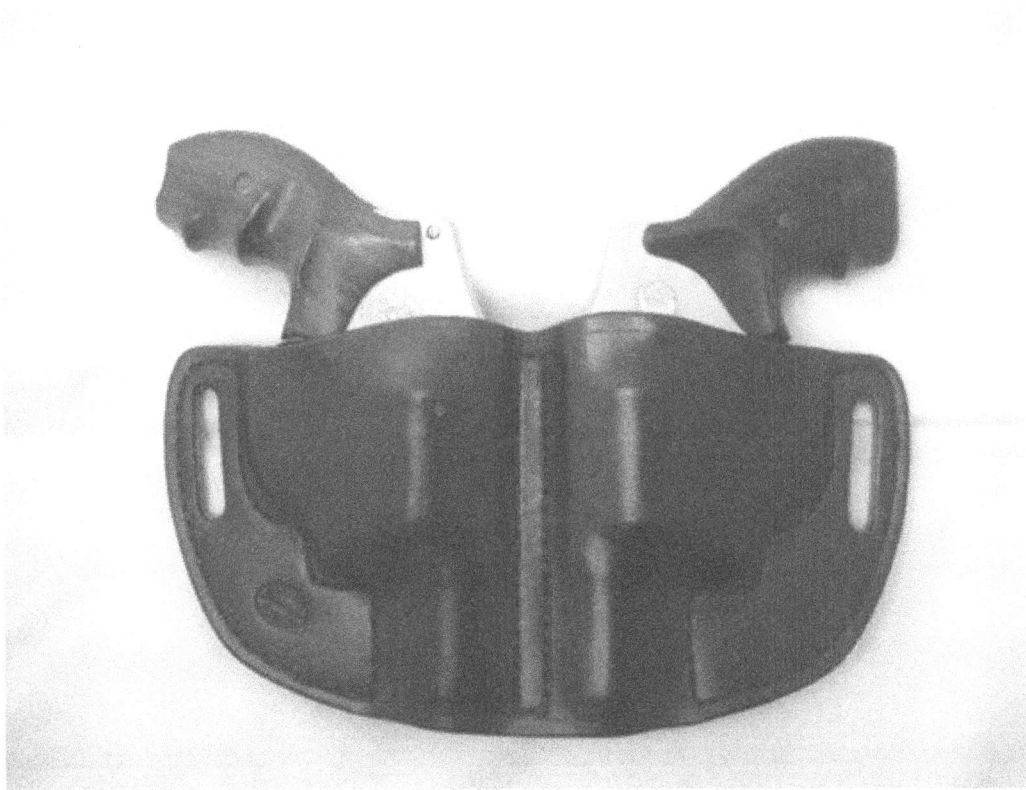

J Frame Holster New York Reload by
by Bell Charter Oak

Viper by
De Santis

Beautiful offerings by DM Bullard

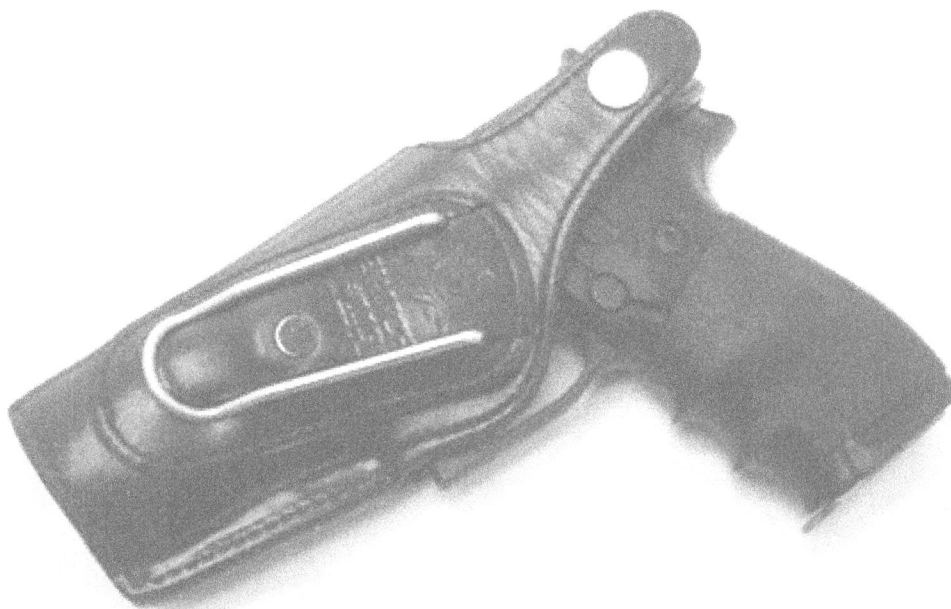

Bianchi Talon, a 20 year old design
that still works perfectly

Magazine pouches by
Aker and Sam Andrews

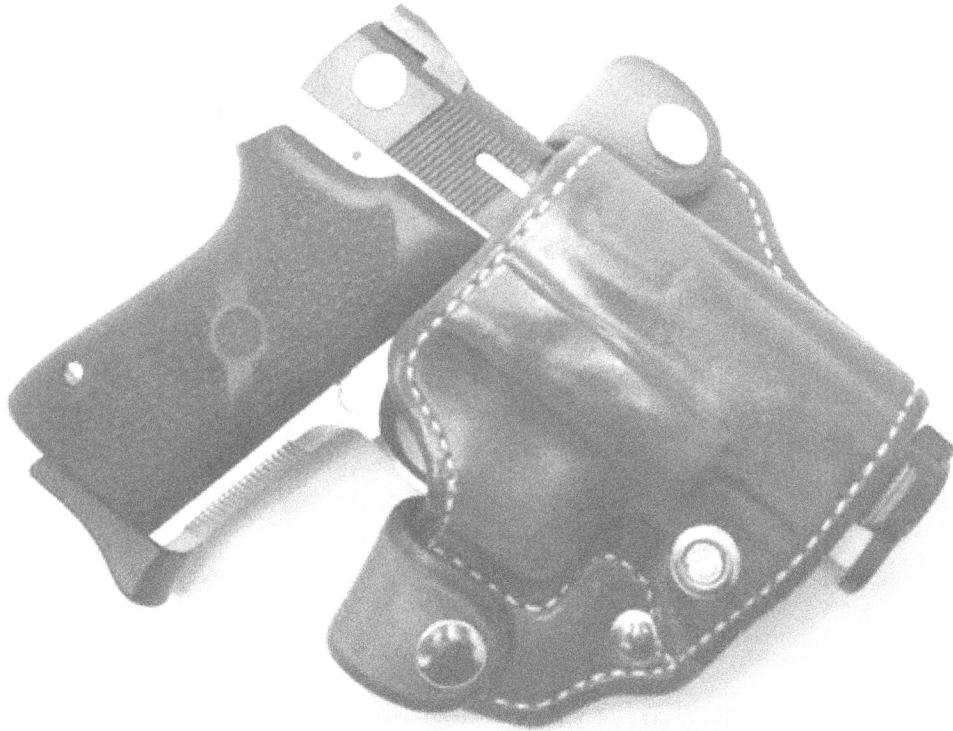

The newest offering by Sam Andrews,
You can remove it without
taking off your belt

Galco Executive Shoulder Holster
for the Walther PPK. The only way to carry
while wearing a tuxedo.
Photo credit: Galco

A Heckler and Koch Briefcase with
Heckler and Koch MP5K
Submachine gun in 9mm NATO

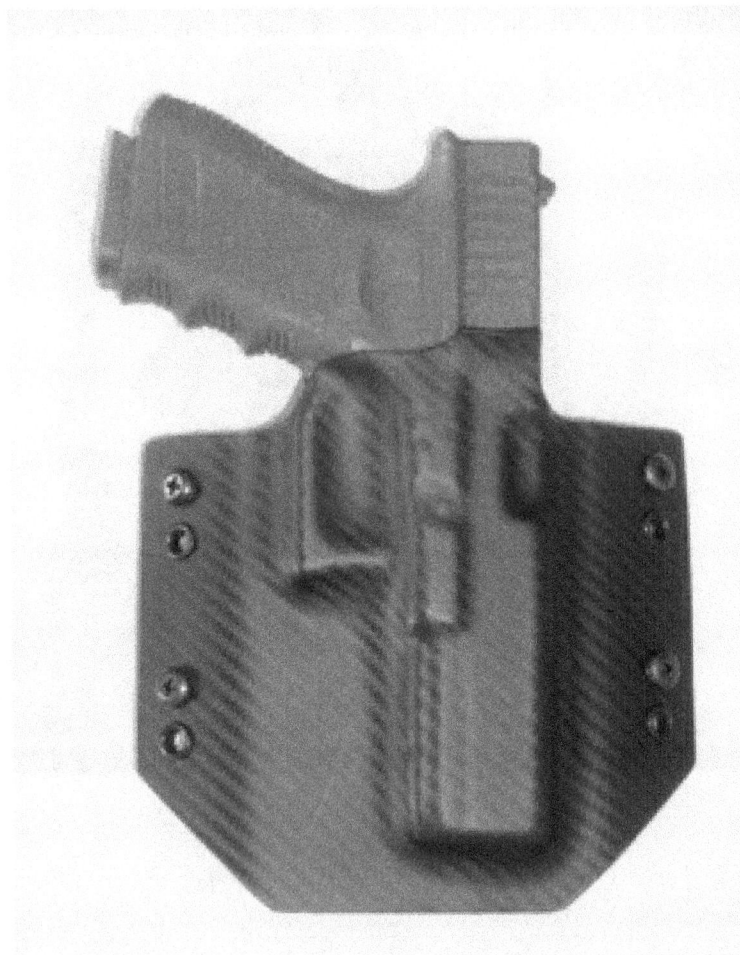

Crossfire Holsters
Kydex holster

(Photo Credit: Michael Weissberg)

Coffman Concealment Concepts
Kydex holster
(Photo Credit: Michael Weissberg)

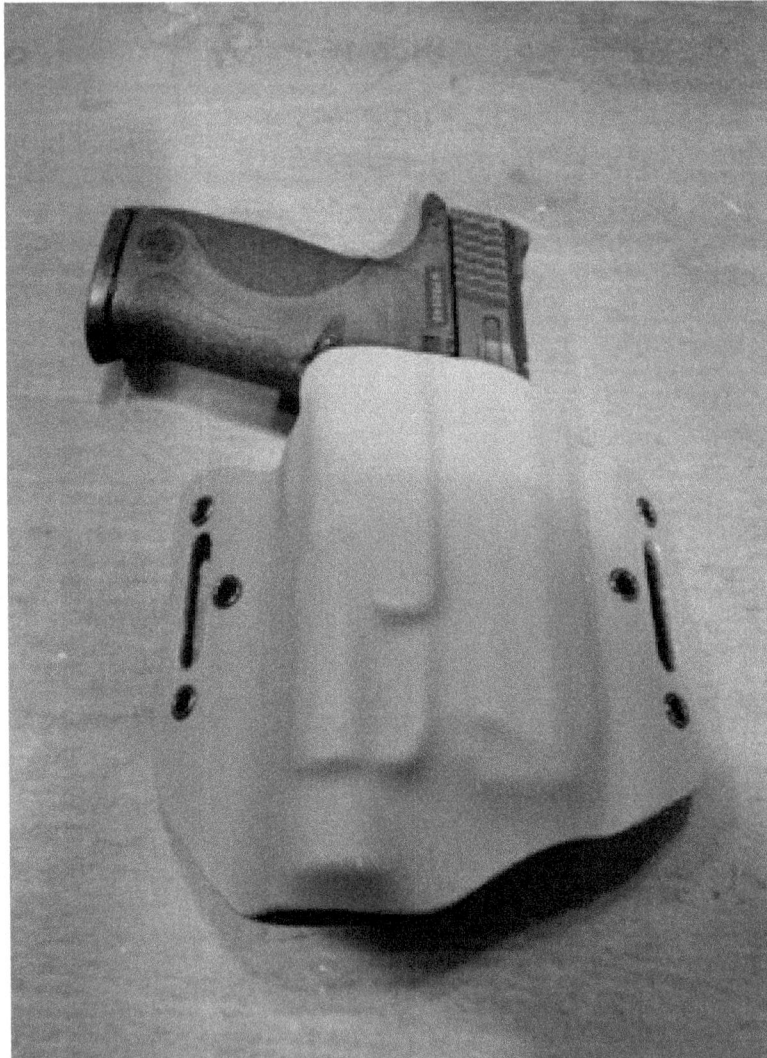

Coffman Concealment Concepts
Kydex holster with light
(Photo Credit: Michael Weissberg)

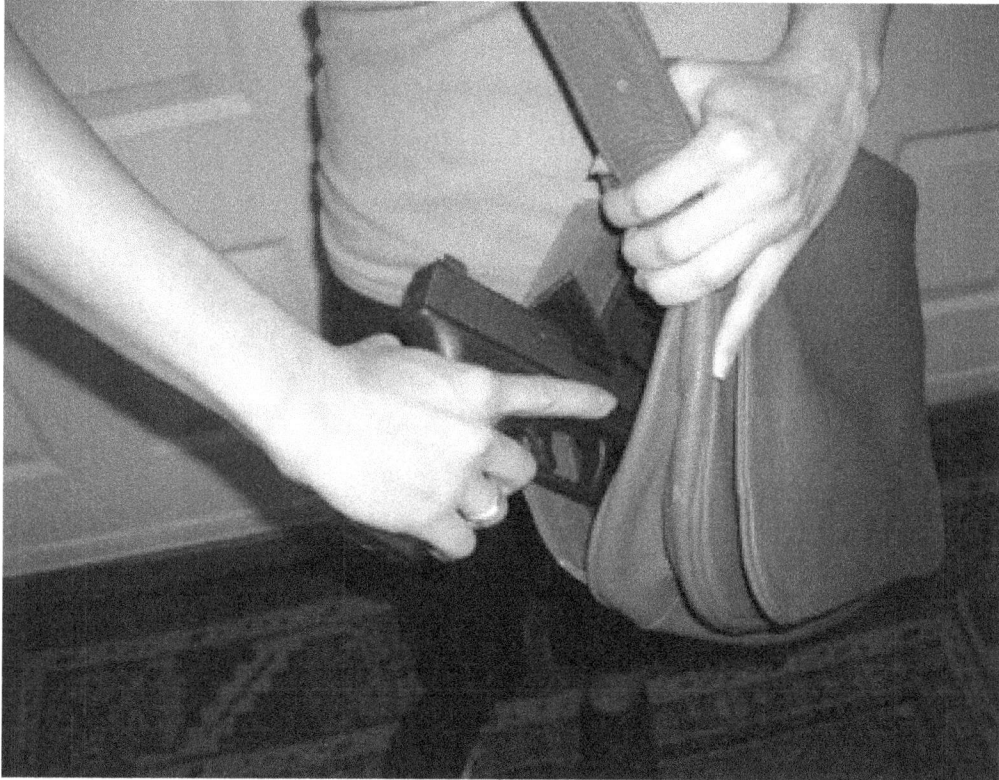

Holster Purse from
Coronado Leather
(Photo Credit: Michael Weissberg)

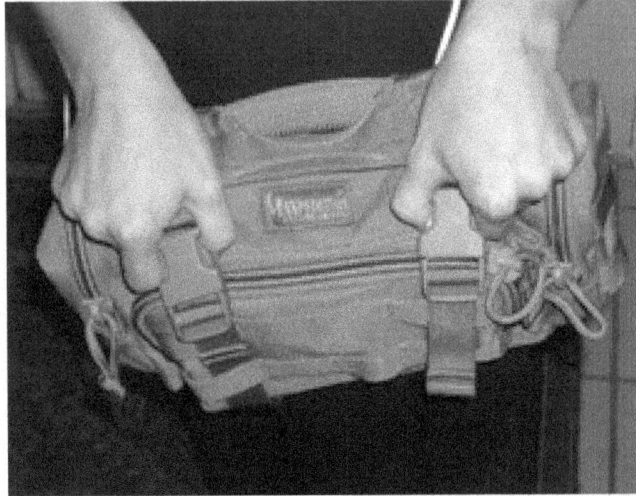

Holster waist pack
Maxpedition
(Photo Credit: Michael Weissberg)

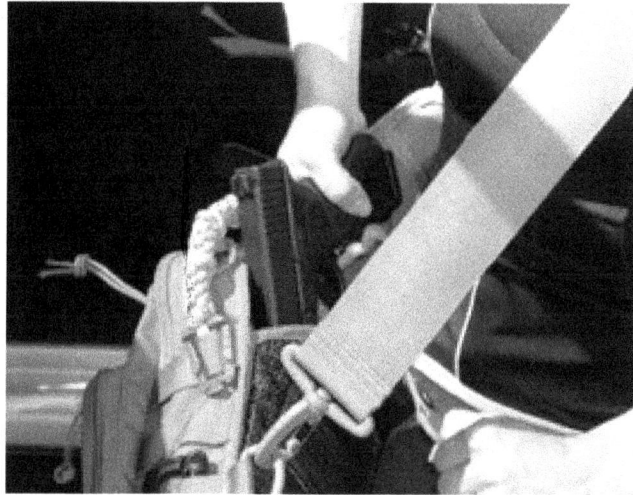

Holster backpack
Maxpedition
(Photo Credit: Michael Weissberg)

Holster backpack
Maxpedition
(Photo Credit: Michael Weissberg)

Holster backpack
Maxpedition

(Photo Credit: Michael Weissberg)

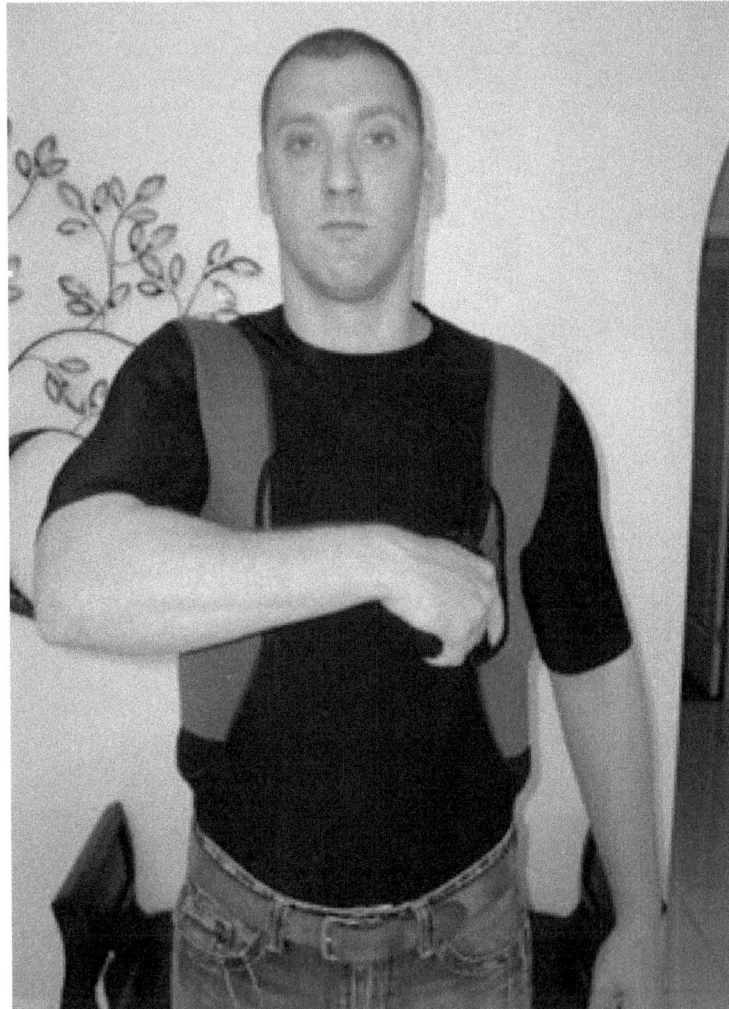

Holster shirt

5.11 Tactical

(Photo Credit: Michael Weissberg)

Holster shirt

5.11 Tactical

(Photo Credit: Michael Weissberg)

Holster backpack
Maxpedition
(Photo Credit: Michael Weissberg)

Holster backpack
Maxpedition
(Photo Credit: Michael Weissberg)

Holster backpack
Maxpedition
(Photo Credit: Michael Weissberg)

Holster backpack
Maxpedition
(Photo Credit: Michael Weissberg)

Select Carry Slingpack
5.11 Tactical

(Photo Credit: Michael Weissberg)

SWAT Team Operator
Det. Sgt. Reny Garcia Deploys HK MP5K
Select Carry Slingpack
5.11 Tactical

(Photo Credit: Michael Weissberg)

SWAT Team Operator
Det. Sgt. Reny Garcia Deploys HK MP5K
Select Carry Slingpack
5.11 Tactical

(Photo Credit: Michael Weissberg)

Holster backpack

Maxpedition

(Photo Credit: Michael Weissberg)

VS

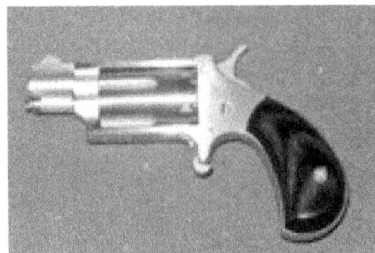

Concealability: Is what you give up
worth the savings in size?
Comparative Pistol Sizes
Glock 24 (top) 8.85"
Glock 35 (Bottom) 8.15"
Photo credit: Michael Weissberg

Concealability: Is what you give up
worth the savings in size?
Comparative Pistol Sizes
Glock 22 (top) 7.32"
Glock 23 (Middle) 6.85"
Glock 26 (Bottom) 6.29"
Photo credit: Michael Weissberg

Concealability: Is what you give up
worth the savings in size?
Comparative Pistol Sizes
Glock 18 (Top) 9"
Glock 22 (Bottom) 7.32"
Photo credit: Michael Weissberg

Concealability: Is what you give up
worth the savings in size?
Comparative Pistol Sizes
Glock 22 (top) 7.32"
Glock 26 (Bottom) 6.29"
Photo credit: Michael Weissberg

Glock 26 Suppressed
With Gemtech Aurora Approx. 9.6"

Glock 22
With Mako Foregrip
Class III/Title 2
Approx. 7.6"

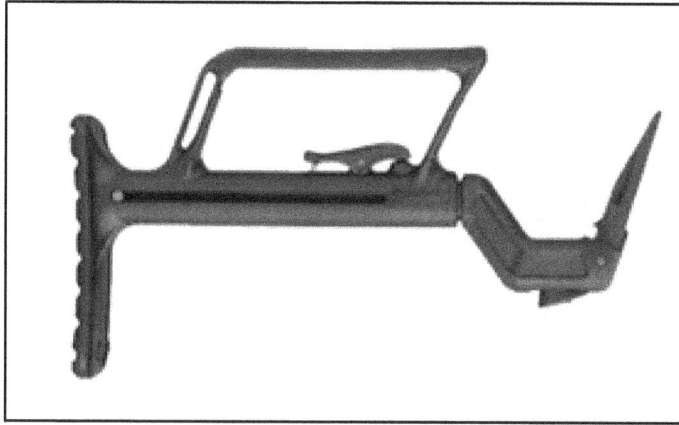

Mako Stock
Class III/Title 2

Glock 22
With Mako Foregrip
And Mako Stock
Class III/Title 2

FAB Defense K.P.O.S Pistol to PDW Conversion
Class III/Title 2

EMA Tactical Roni Glock SBR Conversion
Class III/Title 2

Legal Weapons of Opportunity and Blunt Weapons

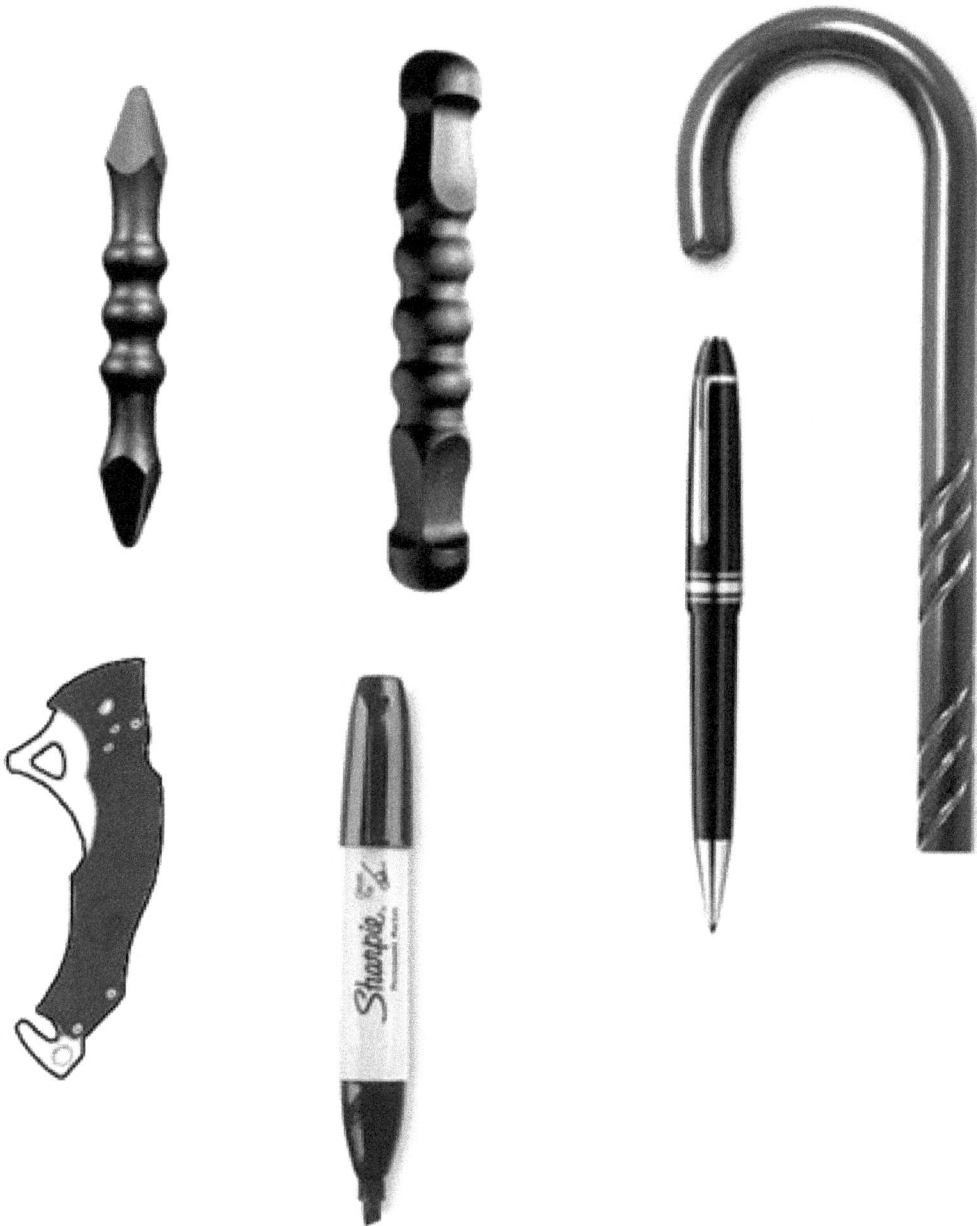

A mini expandable baton.
ASP used to make these; now there
are only knockoffs available.
Photo credit: Bram Frank

Cold Steel Pocket Shark

Sharpie Stainless Steel Permanent Marker

A sharpie can be used as a Kuboton or Yawara stick,
And you can take it on a plane or in the White House

Mont Blanc Le Grand Pen

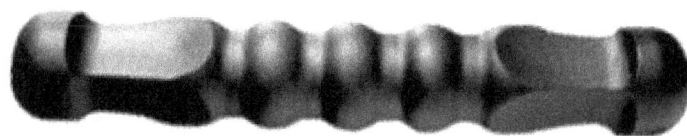

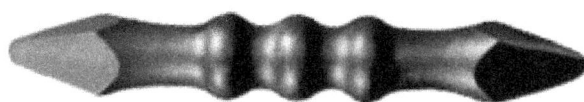

Cold Steel Koga SD1
Mini Koga SD2
This tool combines the teachings of Remy Presas, Wally Jay,
George Dillman, and Bram Frank.

Uzi Pens

Smith and Wesson Tactical Pen
Benchmade Tactical Pen
Schrade Tactical Pen

What the author carries

These next photos show the on-duty and off-duty choices made by the author. Remember, this is one man's opinion, but also remember money was not a factor, since the guns and holsters are for the most part, free.

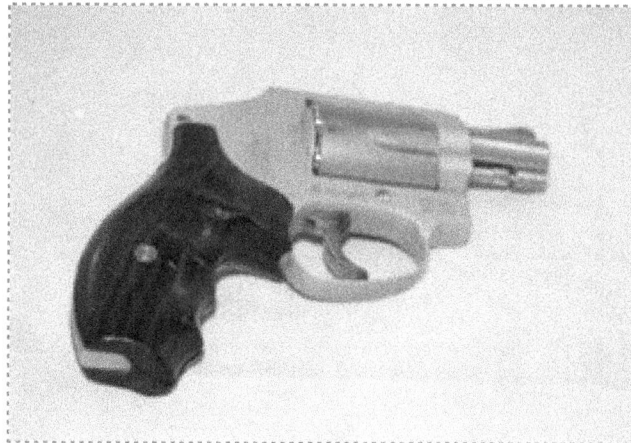

These are the author's guns:
Glock 35
Glock 22
Glock 27
S&W 642
Photo credit: Michael Weissberg

These are the author's guns:
S&W 642 Galco Ankle Glove
Walther PPK/S Galco Ankle Glove
Photo credit: Michael Weissberg

Walther PPK/S Galco shoulder holster
Photo credit: Michael Weissberg

Glock 35 and Glock 22
Glock 22 with Safariland light
Photo credit: Michael Weissberg

Sig 556 Pistol

(Photo Credit: Michael Weissberg)

Draco AK Pistol 7.62 X 39

(Photo Credit: Michael Weissberg)

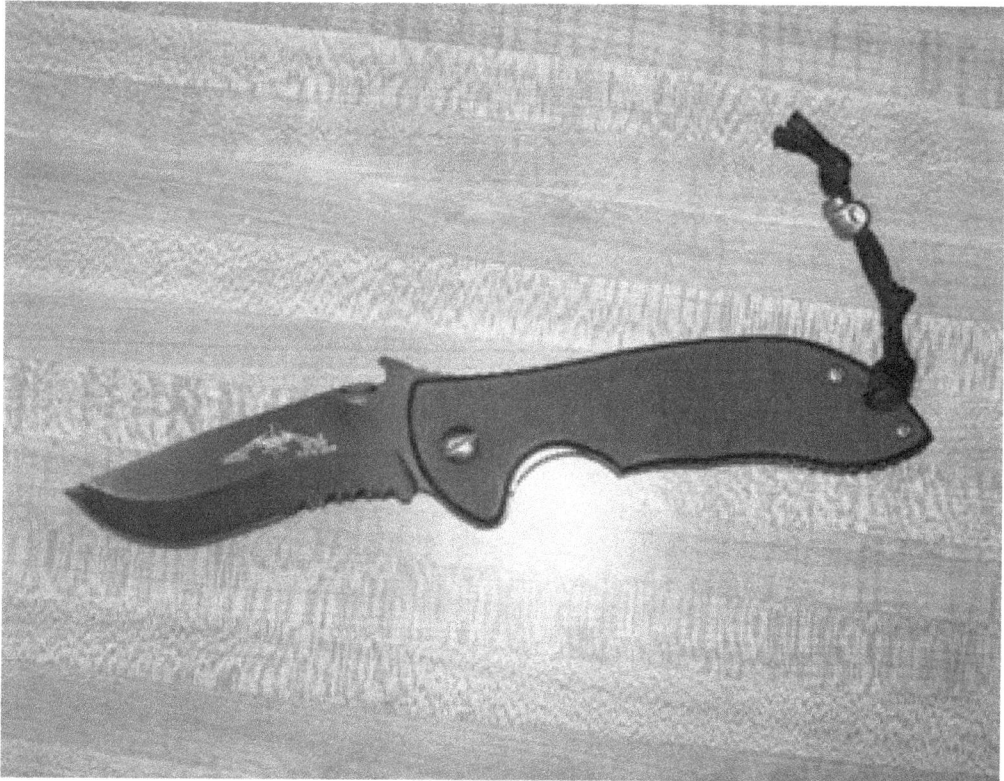

Emerson Commander

(Photo Credit: Michael Weissberg)

Sig P226 .40 with 3 port comp by APW
Factory 20 round Magazine
(Photo Credit: Michael Weissberg)

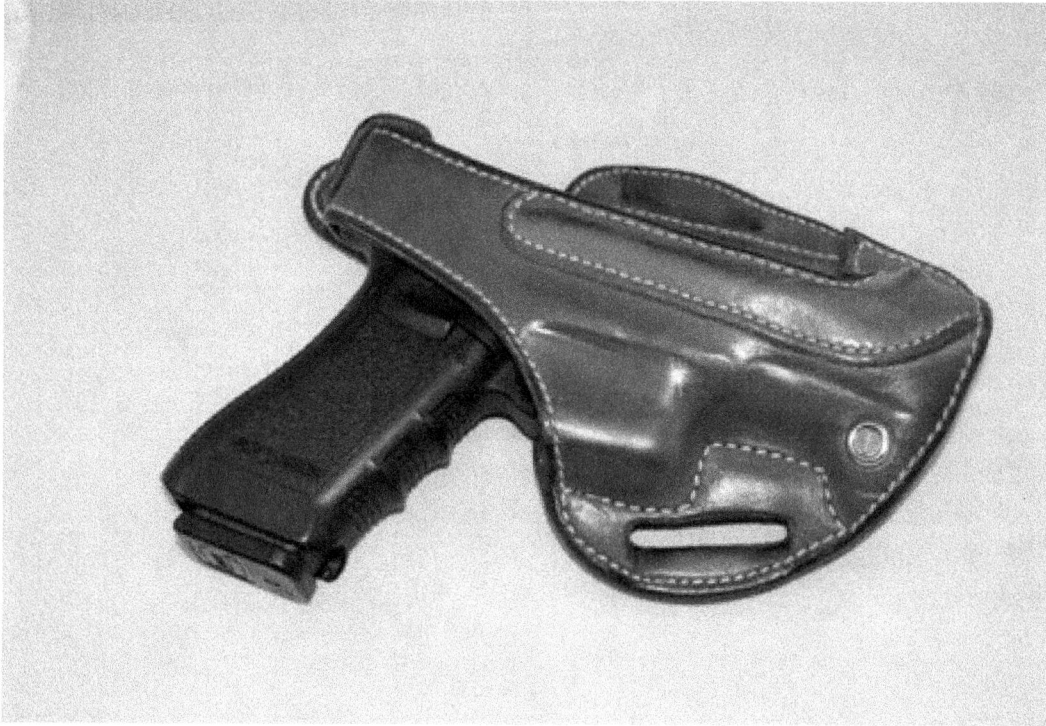

Glock 22 in a Sam Andrews
IPSC Pancake Used For Daily Carry
as a Police Detective
(Photo Credit: Michael Weissberg)

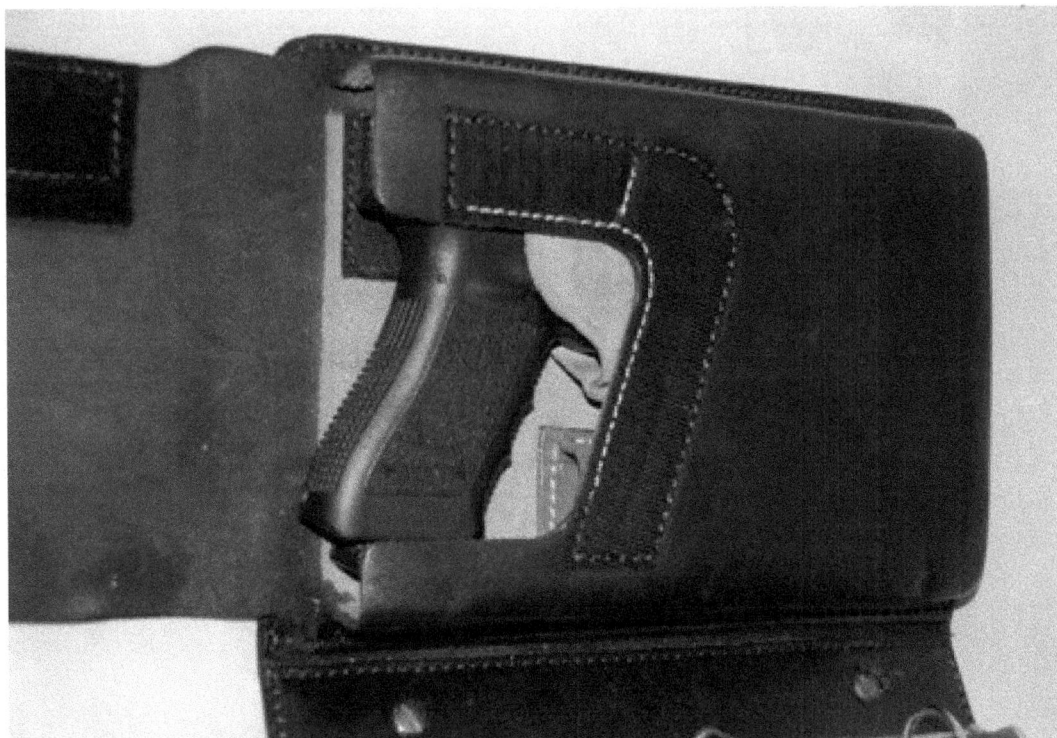

Glock 22 in a Sam Andrews
Notebook Used For Daily Carry
as a Bodyguard
(Photo Credit: Michael Weissberg)

Kydex Neck Holster
Used For Deep Cover
(Photo Credit: Michael Weissberg)

Hellweg Gun Belt
20 years and still going strong!
(Photo Credit: Michael Weissberg)

Every day is a holiday, every formation's a parade, and every paycheck's a fortune!

Police Academy Saying
Michael Weissberg

Do the right thing, at the right time, for the right reason, and the truth will bear you up.

Police Academy Saying
Michael Weissberg

It's a beautiful thing we're doing!

Police Academy Saying
Michael Fiscaletti

"Tous les jours à tous points de vue je vais de mieux en mieux"
"Every day in every way I am getting better and better"

Émile Coué

NOTES

NOTES

NOTES

NOTES

NOTES